YOU ARE NOT ALONE

My Escape from a Narcissist to Find Myself Again

ANNIE CHANDLER

First published by Ultimate World Publishing 2025
Copyright © 2025 Annie Chandler

ISBN

Paperback: 978-1-923583-28-3
Ebook: 978-1-923583-29-0

Annie Chandler has asserted her rights under the Copyright, Designs and Patents Act 1988 to be identified as the author of this work. The information in this book is based on the author's experiences and opinions. The publisher specifically disclaims responsibility for any adverse consequences which may result from use of the information contained herein. Permission to use information has been sought by the author. Any breaches will be rectified in further editions of the book.

All rights reserved. No part of this publication may be reproduced, stored in or introduced into a retrieval system, or transmitted in any form, or by any means (electronic, mechanical, photocopying, recording or otherwise) without the prior written permission of the author. Any person who does any unauthorised act in relation to this publication may be liable to criminal prosecution and civil claims for damages. Enquiries should be made through the publisher.

Cover design: Ultimate World Publishing
Layout and typesetting: Ultimate World Publishing
Editor: Marnae Kelley
Cover Image Copyright: Cristina Conti-Shutterstock.com

Ultimate World Publishing
Diamond Creek,
Victoria Australia 3089
www.writeabook.com.au

A Note from the Author

―――――――――― ◆◇◆ ――――――――――

Disclaimer:

Expressions of innocence or guilt are my opinion and are backed by actual life events I have lived. I have deliberately obscured some identifying features of the characters in this book, for both legal and moral reasons. I do not presume to tell the story of others who feature prominently in this book. Their feelings, emotions, thoughts and memories are their own. And their names have been changed.

In telling my story, I am cognisant that I write my story and those who have given me permission to recall snippets of theirs. They deserve respect in their own right. Mostly, this is my perspective and the recollection of events that happened to me.

I am not a psychologist, psychiatrist or therapist, so the suggestions I have given are what worked for me to

YOU ARE NOT ALONE

help me escape my narcissistic partner and rebuild my life. These are by no means all the strategies that can or should be used by others.

This book may trigger painful memories and/or unusual reactions. If this occurs, please seek help. At the back of the book, there are contact details of services available.

Dedication

To my children...

I'm sorry for so many things in my life, but never you. You are what kept me going when my light was dim and my spirit was weak.

I am sorry for the times you may have needed more from me than I was able to give, for not being fully present.

The truth is, there were parts of me that were broken, sometimes even shattered. Unfortunately, sometimes you needed to be the stronger of us.

It was never that I didn't love you. Never that. I love you, wholly and completely.

It was because I didn't and couldn't love myself. But that's not okay. I'll spend the rest of my life becoming the mother you deserved from the start.

All my love and gratitude,

Mumma xoxoxo

For those who have walked the same path... I hope you find hope in this book, and the strength to make the important decisions, whatever they mean for you, to find a better place for yourself. I am with you in spirit.

Much love,

Annie xx

Testimonials

You Are Not Alone was openly and honestly portrayed by Annie. It highlights the anguish, pain and embarrassment many of us are forced to endure from another's behaviour in a narcissistic relationship. Congratulations, my beautiful sister, for showing us all how to stand up for what is right, as well as encouraging others to join together to help those in need. **SA**

This is a raw, powerful but hopeful book that shifts from simply surviving to actively rebuilding and reclaiming yourself. The honesty in admitting how close Annie came to giving up, then turning that into a call for resilience, will hit home for anyone who has ever felt the same darkness. This takes bravery and tenacity to achieve this. **DS**

What can I say? This book is as insightful as it gets in describing something so cruelly inflicted on Annie by her narcissistic partner. I found myself both crying and cheering her on as she outlined her difficult journey from where she was to where she is now. Her courage will inspire anyone who reads this amazing book. **MR**

YOU ARE NOT ALONE

From reading the introduction of Annie's book, *You Are Not Alone*, I realised that sharing our bad experiences is the only way to heal. No one wants to see the word 'RAPE' at the beginning of a written work, but how can we use any other one to describe this horrific experience. We can no longer pussyfoot around. This word needs to be said and heard. Thank you, Annie, for sharing your story. It will continue to heal you, and definitely give others hope they can heal, too. **WD**

Contents

A Note from the Author	iii
Dedication	v
Testimonials	vii
Introduction	1
Chapter 1: Where I Was to Where I Am Now	7
Chapter 2: Don't Go There	19
Chapter 3: Why Am I Attracted to Bad Boys?	31
Chapter 4: The Shit's Hit the Fan	43
Chapter 5: You've Got This, Girlfriend!	55
Chapter 6: Let's Break It Down	67
Chapter 7: I'M Screwed Up… BIG TIME	81
Chapter 8: I'm So Pretty, Oh So Pretty… NOT	91
Chapter 9: Vomit Out the Hate – It's Cathartic	103
Chapter 10: I'm on My Way to Loving Life Again	113
Chapter 11: Wash Away the Dirt and Love Me, Warts and All	125
Chapter 12: It's a Wrap	137
Conclusion	151
References	155
Acknowledgements	161
Author Biography	165
Annie's Book Nook	167
Help Services in Australia	169

Introduction

> *Our brains are wired for connection, but trauma rewires them for protection. That's why healthy relationships are difficult for wounded people.*
> Ryan North, www.themindsjournal.com

He RAPED me.

My narcissistic ex-partner, who we will call Arse, did it to me when I was asleep. He'd often spoon, using his right arm to trap me like a fly in a spider's web. When Arse saw the evidence, the blood on the sheets, me in a state of shock and huddled on the end of the bed, his response was *'I was asleep, so it's not really rape.'* I've got news for you. It was, and it is!

To add insult to injury, Arse didn't offer to take me to the doctor or the hospital, which was certainly needed. He looked at his watch, grabbed his gym bag and indicated he was late. This left me alone, knowing if I went to the hospital and they saw what my injury was, they would be required to do a rape test and document evidence, whether I was going to report it or not. I thought Arse loved me. He said he did. I loved him, so I chose not to go that route. Instead, I showered, did my best to dress the wound, and then stripped the bed. I didn't wash those sheets. They went in the bin, along with any feelings and emotions. I learned to wear a colourful mask in public, like those in Venice at the annual Carnivale.

And that's when the black dog and I became friends. I was already taking a low dose of antidepressants. When I finally saw my doctor, who happened to be Arse's as well, the doctor was amazed I was there alone, because Arse wanted to be at all appointments. I was also looking so unkempt and gaunt. I had dropped weight and was fifty-seven kilograms by then. The last time I weighed that, I was pre-pubescent.

I told no one, especially my children. How could I place that burden on them? I was ashamed that I had been blind-sided. A person with a university degree doesn't automatically have the insight to know when they are being played. Arse seemed harmless enough, even simple in many ways, but I learned this was a facade

INTRODUCTION

covering his real character. He was manipulative, and I was his puppet.

Four months later, my cousin, Ali, who I call my sister, suggested we get together as she was worried about me. Arse wasn't happy I wanted to go without him as a chaperone. This is when I saw another side, a more aggressive part of his personality, aimed at me. It was a great relief to get away from such a constrictive lifestyle. I was in denial. I lived like a hermit. When Ali realised what had happened and why he was asking for some personal information, she twigged he had engaged a lawyer. After I returned home, she organised for me to stay with her in Queensland for another holiday and had a barrister friend talk with me. He went through Arse's and my financial details and believed it should be a 50/50 split, or at least 45/55, with me having the 45%.

On my return, I learned Arse had indeed engaged a lawyer. However, he was also on the search for my replacement and had been on at least one date.

I had moved into the spare bedroom shortly after the rape and had a full suitcase behind the door when I was in the room so I'd have time to call for help should he try to enter. I only used the bathroom when Arse was out of the house, and I knew he'd be a while, laughing and enjoying being social in the lifestyle village we'd only recently bought into. They are a gossip pit. With everyone only hearing his side of the story and not knowing me at all, I quickly knew whose side they were on.

Not once did he ask me how I was. He refused to discuss it as he believed it was 'old news', though interestingly enough, I have recorded his confession. This is what I used to turn the tables in my favour. I accepted 30/70 in the separation deal, which my lawyer thought was bonkers. However, I was free... from him and where it happened. I knew I could rebuild my life and that any time, I could take the recording to the police and have him charged. That is the ultimate revenge—him always wondering if or when I'll play my ace.

That's my story. It is no worse nor better than anyone else's. Trauma is trauma. It takes its toll, emotionally, physically and psychologically. It wrecks lives like a tornado. You can choose to rebuild, however.

Writing, talking or admitting something that has happened requires a leap of faith you probably were not previously ready to take. That's okay. You need to do it in your own time.

However, believe me when I say that once that journey to self-love commences, there is no turning back. There are often speed bumps so huge your suspension will be wonky for a while, potholes you could lose your car in and

INTRODUCTION

more detours down windy back roads than you can poke a stick at, but you will get there if you follow this process.

Congratulations on choosing to buy this book. Now read it!

I have been there. I have lived through the trauma. More importantly, I won the battle, and you can too. It does take hard work and returning to events you have pretended to hide away in the back of your mind's filing cabinet. It will hurt more than ripping off a band-aid that is stuck to the scab. It needs to be done, and only you can do it.

> *Trauma creates change you didn't choose. Healing is about creating change you do choose.*
> Michelle Rosenthall, www.mindsetmadebetter.com

Chapter 1

Where I Was to Where I Am Now

───────◆◇◆───────

> *I read a truth that carved itself into my bones... "The ones who love the hardest are the ones who break the quietest." And I felt the silence of every night I've spent piecing myself together.*
> www.facebook.com/narcissisticabusesurvivors

Depression is more than just feeling sad or low. At its basic level, it affects how individuals think, feel and function daily, and its effects can manifest in various ways. These lead to disturbances in your personal life and your ability to function effectively at work and in your social relationships. This is because the emotional well-being of a person is damaged, and they often feel persistent sadness, feelings of hopelessness and low self-esteem. Their belief and the ability to love themselves have been stripped away. Their self-worth no longer exists. This has an impact that impairs cognitive functions, causing difficulty concentrating, making decisions and retaining memory. These symptoms often make performing everyday tasks or maintaining healthy relationships challenging, at the very least.

I ticked the box for every one of these. Getting 100% in a test for depression is not an achievement you want to brag about. I had a total loss of confidence in most everyday things and totally second-guessed myself. I had previously travelled Europe and the UK alone, managing to book flights, hotels, tours and the like, but was then unable to do anything that required me to think and act with any great degree of motivation.

I have little recollection of much for about six months after the rape. I do know that my 'sister,' my cousin Ali, with whom I'm very close, was the person who got me to open up to talk about everything. She was so concerned and knew something had happened to me. Within weeks, I was in Brisbane with her. She had organised for me to see a barrister friend of hers to discuss what she believed Arse had already planned, and she was correct. While I was away in Hobart with her about three weeks earlier, he had visited his accountant and the company where the money from his self-managed super fund was invested. Even with this evidence, I was still under the illusion that it would all disappear. Guess what... it didn't. I was hiding from the world, but worse, I was hiding from myself.

Quite often, the physical effects of depression are underestimated, which further exacerbates the individual's mental health. Many experience fatigue, sleep disturbances and changes in appetite or weight. Chronic pain, headaches and/or migraines and gastrointestinal issues may also affect an individual, making life even more complicated than the cause.

Once again, I was an overachiever. Some days, I could hardly get out of bed, didn't want to get out of bed, as I would have to think and feel, which hurt my mind, heart and soul. Sleep was very much a hit-or-miss affair. I was tired, so tired I wanted to cry, but I couldn't fall asleep. If I did, it was for very short periods, and I often woke to my heart beating way too fast from fear.

Nothing tempted me to eat. When I did, I usually felt nauseous. Foods I had craved previously did nothing for my appetite. It was as if my taste buds had gone on a holiday. Even my addiction to coffee was almost non-existent. I weighed in at 64 kilograms after losing nearly 30 kilograms after my gastric sleeve surgery. Four months after the rape, I was a gaunt 57 kilograms. I saw healthier corpses when I worked for a funeral director. My gastric reflux became worse, even though I was eating so little. I was prescribed Somac 20 mg once a day but lived on Mylanta and Gaviscon tablets in between. I kept both those companies afloat for a couple of years.

And I ached, physically ached. I felt a heaviness, even though I was lighter than I had been since my pre-teen years. My body didn't seem to want to function, to move. I had suffered from migraines, generally associated with hormones, which were significantly reduced after my hysterectomy at forty-one years of age. They came back with a vengeance. They hit the left side of my face, and I often experienced auras, as well as a dull ache. My vision was also sometimes affected. It was like looking through a smeared window. So, I didn't read, I didn't write—and for an author, that is not a good sign. In fact, besides documents and emails to my lawyer, I did not write one word, not for my blogs, nor did I continue the novel I had planned and started to write. It is still in a folder on my computer, and I will get back to it... someday. My writing was put on hold for over two years. I didn't even keep a journal as I had done, religiously. At a time when you'd think you would bare your soul, writing it down as a form of therapy, I couldn't. I wouldn't because that would make it all too real. And I wasn't ready to own it at that time. I was the proverbial ostrich with its head buried deeply in the sand.

The true area of torment for me was that my depression often led me to withdraw from social interactions. I would cancel coffee catchups, lunches and movie nights with friends at the last moment with some really lame excuses, worse than a book of Dad jokes. It meant I would have to get up, shower, dress and leave my bedroom, my only safe place in the house. It was all too difficult. Even when I longed for this contact, I knew I could not contribute to a discussion. Besides, who would want an Eeyore as part of the group? This strained my friendships because my friends were unaware of what I was experiencing or what caused it. And I couldn't tell them. I had no words to explain it all. For a person who is usually quite eloquent, I could barely string a sentence together, let alone have it make sense.

As for family, no one knew my secret for months, except for Ali. I couldn't do that to my children. A mother is supposed to be strong, to know what to do in any situation, and I was usually that person. I felt ashamed, even though I was not guilty of the rape. I wore that shame like a cloak. It covered me and my emotions and protected the three greatest gifts I brought into life. I didn't think I had any other choice. Besides not having the strength to go through the process of charging Arse with rape, the court case, etc., I didn't need them to be associated with what I considered my shame. It's amazing what your mind thinks of, ably nudged in that direction by who I now know to be a covert, passive-aggressive narcissist.

I also struggled to maintain my responsibilities at home. I didn't clean the house, except for my toilet and the shower I had to share; my fear of germs was heightened at this time, leading to feelings of guilt and inadequacy. These challenges only created a vicious cycle that deepened my depression. And my self-care was almost non-existent at times. Why would I want to get out of bed and shower? I lived in pjs, or clothes that made me less attractive— track pants or leggings, t-shirts and hoodies. I wore no makeup, and my hair was often oily and messy. Basically, I didn't take pride in my appearance, which was extremely unusual. I was a woman who lived for her monthly beauty salon treatments, regular hair appointments for highlights and visits to the nail salons for pedicure and manicure treatments. I'm not even sure how regularly I changed my bedding, though because I was in bed so much and my personal hygiene was random, the sheets probably should have been changed more frequently than usual, not less!

It was easy to hide from the world. Arse and I had only moved into an over-55s village a couple of months before his assault. While I spent time unpacking, he spent time socialising. Therefore, by the time things turned to shit, I was basically a non-entity. So, who would they believe when he broadcast loud and wide what a gold-digger I was?

For my own mental health, it was easier for me to make an offer way below what I should have received. I used the threat of going to the police with his taped confession to get him to sign the documents, which allowed me, once they went through the necessary channels, to walk away with very little of our joint property... but with my freedom. It was enough to buy me a unit four hundred kilometres away and a car and to put some away for retirement, but very little. I had to go back to work. I found this a struggle, even after lots of therapy, as I needed to interact daily with people I didn't know. I had taught for nearly forty years, but returning to the classroom was like starting over as a first-year teacher in a country town away from family and friends. It was daunting; I often questioned my ability to do something I would normally do, 'flying by the seat of my pants.' I examined everything I did and suffered great anxiety in a classroom of six students. I doubted my ability as a teacher. I felt a fraud. Therefore, I spent much time with the students practising mindfulness and breathing techniques... more for my benefit than theirs. Fortunately, I had free rein of the class program!

Four years on, and I'm doing okay. It's probably better than okay, though sometimes it seems like I backtrack a little. I have begun to appreciate many of the activities I used to enjoy, such as going to movies and the theatre, eating out with friends, or even just having a coffee at a café by myself. It's even better if it is close to the beach, which I love. The waves soothe this tortured soul. It was one of the reasons I chose the town I did.

I found a group of over-60s who met for a coffee once a month. It was like walking off a mountain making myself attend the first catch-up, but I was so pleased I did. I met an extraordinary, vibrant and friendly lady, Chrissy, who ensured I had her mobile number. We will be friends for life.

I remember the first time I laughed, really laughed. It stopped me immediately because I hadn't heard that sound in a long time. I realised I was having 'happy' moments, and that was an uplifting part of my recovery. Being diagnosed with PTSD is not something I would have thought of. Fortunately, I had help from therapists, but I am also determined by nature. I started to read everything I could about the subject and other areas, such as the vagus nerve. It's an amazing machine, our body. However, if something goes wrong in one area with depression, PTSD and so on, it's like removing that one stick from the game of Pick-Up Sticks I played as a child, and everything falls in a heap. Basically, you're in this messy heap with no way to get back up.

Fortunately, I made it out of bed and off the floor. Four years on from the rape I am healthy... probably put on a little too many kilos, but meh, I feel better with a bit of padding. I am the best I have been for years, even pre-rape, because living with Arse was a heavy burden to carry. I have reduced my depression medication through practising daily mindfulness rituals to help me stay positive and focused, and I have a calmness I've never had previously. I won't say every day has been a picnic; however, I can usually work around the ups and downs to keep a relatively even keel.

My biggest positive was that I started to journal again. Not often, and it was mainly meaningful things I had read on Facebook or quotes I sourced from the internet. I'd copy them and print them out, stick them in my journal and decorate them. I'm no artist, so it was usually stickers I had from my teaching days that said, 'You are AWESOME' and 'Love yourself,' etc., which I stuck on as positive affirmations. And I am journalling to this day. That was the stepping stone to start writing again. I found that more difficult and often stared at the monitor, willing words to magically appear. My fingers were poised on the keyboard, ready to type, but my brain wasn't willing to be part of the exercise... a bit like me in a gym!

Eventually, I began doing what I had done over a decade earlier and wrote eight hundred words on a topic from a prompt. I found a website with a hundred writing prompts and randomly chose one every morning. I wrote before I did anything else... except get a coffee. That's my one essential, and I can't function before my caffeine hits. My writing still didn't flow as easily as I had hoped. I equate it to someone who has had a spinal injury and needs to learn to walk again. It was small steps. I'd write anything trying to complete the allotted word count. I was often hopeless with that, so I cut myself some slack. After about a month, I was making significant progress. I'd print out the blogs and file them, in case I could use them sometime. It's amazing what different forms of therapy can achieve.

I knew a lady who had left an abusive partner, another narcissist, and she knitted. I have absolutely no idea how many beanies she had made, but she could have given one to every bald man (or woman) in Australia and still have a box left over. As money was tight, and wool expensive, she'd often bought wool from charity shops, so the beanies were a mismash of colours. I suggested she have a stall and sell them for money to buy more wool. At her first stall, and only charging $5 a beanie, she made over $150. I think that was her therapy turning point. She realised she could do something worthwhile that other people loved and that helped her.

What have I achieved through my process of reclaiming myself? I now have a better sense of self-worth and self-esteem. It will still take time as I was flawed before I met Arse. It's been a battle from my childhood and some trauma there. I'm continuing my journey to self-love using daily affirmations. Plus, I'm more direct when speaking with others. Not in an offensive way, hopefully, but I am no longer the 'yes person' I was. I have my opinions and will share them, rather than accepting those of others to keep the peace.

This is sometimes difficult when you're a Libra woman who doesn't like the scales to be unbalanced! Therefore, it's about challenging yourself to be a better version of you. I'm doing it for myself, not for anyone else.

However, there is a tiny bit of me that wants to *flip the bird* to Arse to show him that he didn't break me. He certainly gave it a very good shot, and the rape wasn't only the time he failed me... but it was the last time I allowed him to tread on me. He neglected me at other times when I should have been taken to either a doctor or the hospital. The rape was the first red cross against him, a fall was the second, followed closely by the damage I did in tearing internal stitches while helping him. Amazingly, he disregarded all of these as nothing.

Well, mate, I'll tell you something for free... 'three strikes and you're out.'

> *The most challenging part of healing is understanding that I was responsible for my closure. It had to come from within. It's even more difficult when I knew I had been betrayed by someone I thought loved me. Ultimately, it's a catch-22 situation. I needed to let them know how much he hurt me, physically and mentally; however, my peace and closure can only come when I'm ready to let go of the hatred I hold inside.*
> Annie Chandler, 22 February, 2025,
> www.anniechandlerauthor.com

Chapter 2

Don't Go There

—————— ♦◇♦ ——————

A narcissist doesn't love anyone, they manipulate.

They don't seek healing, just safe places to return to when things go left. They use their past as a crutch, expecting pity while repeating the same toxic cycles. You could pour every ounce of love into them, and they'd still have a backup plan. ...

A narcissist thrives in chaos they create but never take responsibility for. They will twist your words, distort reality, and gaslight you until you question your own sanity. They position themselves as victims while you're left to carry the blame, confusion, and emotional wreckage... What feels like love in the

YOU ARE NOT ALONE

beginning—intense connection, admiration, and passion—is actually grooming for control. ...

Their apologies are not about remorse—they're about convenience... But the cycle repeats—love bombing, devaluation, and discard—leaving you a shell of the person you once were.

And the cruellest part? They often seem charming to others. To the outside world, they wear a mask so convincing, you're the one who seems irrational. You're the one who looks unstable after months or years of emotional erosion.

A narcissist doesn't want love... And no matter how much you give, it will never be enough. Because deep down, they're not looking for someone to love. They're looking for someone to dominate, to use, and ultimately, to blame.

Save yourself. Leave before you forget who you are.

www.facebook.com/silentwritings, May 28 2025

This writing brilliantly sums up what a narcissist is. I wish I had read it years ago and I may have stopped making the same mistakes with different partners because of my personality type... the carer, the giver. It's amazing that once you realise a narcissist's traits, you spot them in others... even women. In fact, women account for 25% of narcissists. There could be a higher percentage of women narcissists, but men usually don't like to admit they are the pawns in the relationship, the ones mistreated and controlled.

I didn't know what a narcissist was until Arse. And it was only because of the rape that, after lots of therapy and reading to help me, I realised he fitted the category of a covert, passive-aggressive narcissist. There are lots of different types.

Narcissists come from all walks of life. As I did, a lot of people assume they are from the lower or working class. Wrong... many are in the middle and upper classes as well, and in all professions. Numerous have leadership roles because they *'talk the talk and walk the walk.'* The origin of this phrase comes from the Shakespeare play *Richard III*, first performed in 1594. It's all a part of their game. Think of some of your bosses, maybe someone in your group of friends who always organises things to work for themselves. Then there are the politicians... especially some current and past world leaders. I'm sure I don't have to name any there!

Some narcissists profess to be religious, but their actions speak more than their beliefs. I have a friend who separated from her husband, a reverend. No one knew what went on behind the rectory door until she left. It took a while before she confided in her friends, and we were horrified. He wasn't a God-fearing man... he was Satan. Fortunately, her faith saved her, in more ways than one. He is no longer in the Church. Sad to say, he is not the only Christian I know who doesn't practise what they preach.

There are many unmistakable signs of narcissism; however, these ten are generally considered the main ones, particularly of those who are overt.

A narcissist...
1. craves attention from you
2. lacks empathy, neither caring about nor trying to understand your feelings
3. has a sense of entitlement, believing you should care for them
4. are masters at manipulating behaviours, using you to achieve their own goals
5. can be charming and engaging—a façade to trap you, like a hunter looking for easy prey
6. rarely take responsibility for their actions, shifting the blame onto you
7. idolises you one moment for show, then devalues you the next... confusing you

8. seeks to control situations and people without any thought or regard for your thoughts and feelings
9. loves to dominate discussions; if you interrupt, you are often belittled, laughed at or provoked for having a different opinion
10. disregards social rules and boundaries as they believe these do not apply to them

Do you know anyone who has several or all of these characteristics?

On the other side of the coin, some narcissists have major problems interacting with others, lacking the necessary social skills. They easily become angry or impatient when things aren't going their way, especially if there are changes. Therefore, they have difficulty controlling their emotions and behaviour. Their understanding of their own feelings about a situation is limited, believing the situation is not due to them. They also experience major problems dealing with stress and often withdraw or avoid situations in which they may be seen as a failure. So, they come across as moody or depressed and have secret feelings of insecurity and shame.

This was Arse to a T. I had to walk around on eggshells and boost his confidence by repeatedly saying how wonderful he was, how well he did things and what a great person he was. I was the fool. He had an excellent opinion of himself, and it certainly helped that he had a younger and, I'll say with some confidence, a good-looking and intelligent woman on his arm.

He didn't have many friends. Arse didn't have the skills to make and keep them. Therefore, it was not surprising he was drawn to a very strong and dominating person, and we, as a couple, regularly socialised with him and his wife. At first, I really enjoyed it, even though Ego, not his name but certainly his nature, was a very heavy drinker. He encouraged Arse to keep up with him and disliked it when I quietly spoke with Arse about slowing down. Ego laughed about 'the ugly side of alcohol'. As I was a non-drinker, I was the chauffeur to events. It's not pleasant when you're the only one who is sober, and the real personalities of the other people emerge during the nights of partying. I slowly learned to dread these as Arse did not realise what an utter fool he was. The worse part was he thought that was the way to behave at other functions, especially family occasions. I could see my friends and children cringe as they wondered about us being such a mismatched pair.

Arse was secretly terrified of showing his flaws and failures. This would destroy the illusion of his superiority, so he'd usually avoided social situations or relationships that did not clearly benefit him. He would communicate his displeasure at me through guilt trips, backhanded compliments or thinly-veiled jokes. He avoided direct communication most of the time, though when he wanted to make a point about something I lacked, Arse wasn't backwards in coming forward. His 'concern' about my weight increased along with the kilos I gained, and he let me know it, usually in front of others.

He needed to be the centre of attention and in control of his partner. This was what definitely happened with his late wife, and I replaced her. As I was the classic carer, I fell right into his web. I didn't see that coming.

It took a few years into our relationship, and me doing relief teaching so I could concentrate on writing, before I felt my control slipping. Arse needed to know where I was going, how long I would be and with whom I was associating. I thought it was lovely, at first, that he would drive me to the event. I'm not sure whether it was because he didn't trust me or because he hated the thought of me going out and having fun without him. Maybe it was a bit of both. Whatever the reason, it certainly changed the dynamics and pleasure of the outing when he invited himself as well, needing to be involved in conversations about which he knew nothing. Often his comments were as embarrassing as his covert remarks about me. I wondered why many of my friends just smiled and kept quiet. They didn't understand what I saw in Arse.

And that's the thing. He was a wonderful person when I met him. He made me dinner one night: steak, mashed potatoes, mixed vegies (frozen) and gravy (from a pack). I thought baked beans on toast was a feast if I didn't have to cook, so this was luxury... and he had a dishwasher! Mind you, it was the only meal he had been taught to cook as he had no home skills whatsoever.

Another time, I had been to the theatre and called in on my way home to tell him about it. Knowing music and theatre were passions of mine, he purchased tickets for us to go and see the 2Cellos. I was touched, especially as the first part of the event was more classic music, and he was just about asleep. Then they ramped it up and played AC/DC's 'Highway to Hell'. You'd have thought he had arranged that himself. He bragged for months about how great he was to take me to the concert. Still, I didn't see the warning signs.

A few months later, I mentioned I was going to Bali for a week in the July school holidays. He suggested he should come so we could see how well we 'lived' together. Little did I know this was an audition! I only learned much later he had been over there previously with another lady, but that didn't work out. Having lived and worked in England for four years after my second divorce, I was used to travelling and doing things by myself. I'd also been to Bali with my family, but I wasn't used to having Arse go everywhere I went. He had massages with me, and reflexology. We went shopping together, walks together, ate out together—though I seemed to be the one who had to choose when and where for everything, which all became too much. I vividly remember stopping in the street, people having to walk around us, while turning to him and saying, 'Will you fucking make one decision... it's not too hard!' This is not like me, and I did feel embarrassed, but I was at the end of my tether. He took offense at this, becoming silent and moody most of the night, and when he spoke and how he spoke to me should have been red flags. Instead, I felt guilty because I had offended him!

Somehow, he also invited himself into joining me on my trip to England. It was where his late wife was born, and they always planned to go there. As it was in the September school holidays, and my rental lease was up around that time, he asked me to move in with him beforehand. It seemed the logical choice as it would help both of us with expenses. Little did I know he was going to cancel the weekly cleaners as he knew what a clean-freak I tended to be, and he just assumed I would take over the cooking. And I did both jobs, while holding down a full-time job. We even drove to work together because we had to travel south of the river and where we worked was only about ten minutes apart. The downside for me was that I arrived at work before 6 am and was often kicked out at 5 pm by the cleaners and had to wait until he finished. It certainly made for a long day because as soon as we arrived home I was the one to start preparing the meal while he showered and kicked back to watch

TV. I should have realised that reruns of *Hogan's Heroes* and the like, instead of the news and something more educational, was another red flag. His house, his TV, his remote!

We purchased a house together—he put my name on the title even though, at that time, I hadn't contributed to it. Then we won LOTTO... just short of one million dollars! The ticket was purchased from our joint savings account, though he was the one who actually bought it while I was paying for our grocery shopping. When he was notified of the win, he went around telling everyone *he* had won lotto... not *we* had! This was just before we moved into the over 55s lifestyle village. We had sold all our old furniture and bought a house full of new stuff. We added a full-length enclosed patio and bought more outdoor lounges and tables. It was during this time that his accountant and the financial advisor from our investment portfolio suggested I should transfer my superannuation into his self-managed super fund. It never really sat well with me, and I felt bullied into it, but it was a done deal. I was tied to Arse tighter than a pig on a spit, and I was slowly being burned.

Then he raped me, barely two months after we had moved into our home, paid for by the lotto win. He kept the money from the sale of the other property, which I thought was fair since he had put up the funds. I did think, however, I should have received something for my furniture that was sold and the sale of all my plants, but I accepted it would go into things for the new place.

Oh, silly, stupid, foolish me. How naïve I was. And many thought he was that. No, my friends... he just acted the fool when it suited him. And that wasn't when it came to separating. He had dollar signs in his eyes and was relentless with his terms. He believed he had paid for the house, even though I had the paperwork to prove that was incorrect. He believed he had paid for the furniture; once again I had the paperwork to prove otherwise. And, by that time we had sold my car, as we agreed we only really required one. That went into buying a brand-new car, over $45,000, with the registration in his name.

At that time, I was still living in the home in the second bedroom, trying to deal with him and the lawyers. It was difficult when I could barely function on a daily basis. It's no wonder it was better to walk away with 30% of the funds, which included my portion of superannuation, and move well away from Perth. I was defeated. And it certainly takes a lot to get me to that place. I was, however, at least in a better place than I had been for over six months, though there was a long way to go.

You didn't lose a loved one—you escaped a toxic nightmare. You broke free from a cycle of abuse, and that takes incredible courage, strength and resilience. Narcissists are incapable of genuine love; they only mimic it to get what they want. To heal, you must accept the truth: you were not loved but used. You were a source of supply, a means to an end and a pawn in their manipulative game. Now you are free to rediscover yourself, embrace true love and live a life filled with purpose, joy and authenticity. You deserve real love, genuine connection and healthy relationships. You deserve to be seen, heard and understood. You deserve to be valued, respected and cherished. Never settle for anything less. You are worthy of love; it will find you when you least expect it.
www.facebook.com/narcissististicabusesurvivors

Chapter 3

Why Am I Attracted to Bad Boys?

---◆◇◆---

> *They know why you're upset. They know why you won't speak to them. They know that they hurt you. Trying to explain things to them only allows them to twist your words, confuse you and bring you back under control. Stop explaining yourself to someone who doesn't care.*
> *www.facebook.com/narcissisticabusesurvivors*

Self-belief is a huge factor in how you perceive yourself and your worth. If you don't believe you are worthy, either consciously or subconsciously, then you attract a specific type of person to you for many reasons. How we are brought up and the situations we find ourselves in at a young age often define how we will be as we get older.

My mother had a narcissistic personality. She was a functional alcoholic and could be viciously cruel when drunk. Although I don't know what her reasons were, she had obviously been through some unspeakable trauma when she was younger, and my siblings and I paid the price. Margie, our mother (but that's what we nicknamed her), had entered the convent twice, though she never took her final vows. I don't think she really knew what she wanted from life, and I believe she only trained as a nurse to appease her parents as they were both in the medical field.

We were a product of poor role models. My parents separated when I was five; basically, my mother just wanted a sperm donor. Had she known about the turkey baster, she may never have had sex the three times she did to fall pregnant with my older sister, my younger brother and me. She would have still married, as she was a good Catholic; however, she was very anti-men and made that known. Once she'd had the children she wanted, she left the marriage.

I was raised in a very Catholic family, so 'Catholic guilt' was a built-in factor. In the Bible, Matthew 7:12, said, *'In everything, then, do to others as you would have them do to you.*' It was constantly drummed into me, both at home and at school, that I shouldn't be selfish. I needed to think pure thoughts, though that was extremely testing when womanhood descended on me in my early teens, and I needed to offer up good acts to God as signs of my contrition.

This wasn't easy when I was living in a warzone most of the time. I had twelve years of Catholic education and even spent my high school years attending my mother's old boarding school as a boarder myself. I found it a relief to be away from the daily turmoil of home life, and at school I could pretend I was a product of a normal family with both parents living together. It was only much later I realised that not all were from 'happy families' there either.

Boy, wasn't it a pleasant and welcoming sight when I went to university and there were males… lots of them! It was almost like being handed a box full of the most exquisite, unique chocolates. I wanted to sample, was tempted to taste, but for years the Catholic guilt and my mother's voice in my head stopped me if I even kissed a boy, let alone explored further the secrets of sex! I lived for the day when I could leave home and see what life was all about.

This is why I think I was attracted to 'bad boys' as they seemed to offer me a taste of what I'd been denied for so long. It was the mid-to-late 1970s, so I drew on my inner bohemian soul and experienced the life most others were living. I'm sorry to say this is where I learned to choose the most unsuitable types who used me for everything. I gave them my heart willingly. I pretended to like their music, mostly heavy metal, when John Denver was my preference. I ran after them with puppy eyes, hanging on their every word, and did things I often didn't want to partake in. Yes, that included marijuana and hashish, drinking and sexual acts I didn't enjoy.

Would you believe I was a teacher at a Catholic school during the week, including teaching religion, while partying on the weekend? It wasn't because I enjoyed it but because I thought it was a means to an end…I'd find love, have a home with the proverbial white picket fence and the children I so desired, so that I could give them the love that had been denied to me by my mother.

Don't get me wrong, I learned to love her. You do when you become a mother yourself, and a single mum at that. You realise how difficult it is to earn a living, and being there for them is a juggle, often with you dropping all the balls at once. I used to say I didn't like my mother, but I loved her because that's what she was. When I became a parent, I told her I loved her. Unfortunately, whatever happened to her when she was younger, she was never able to say it back to me. I knew she loved me in her own way, and in later years she was a wonderful grandmother.

I am the mother I am because I didn't want to be the mother she was.

However, I'm sad to say that wasn't always the case when dating again after divorcing my children's father. I tried to keep my two lives separate, though that didn't always happen.

After my father's death, I learned he annually visited a dominatrix. He clearly felt the need to take out his frustration and angst on a woman, as he was dominated by and had to contend with powerful women in his family. This included my mother, his wife, as well as his mother and his younger, unmarried sister. It was probably his only way to act out his dominance. That's what saddens me the most, the fact that he, too, was looking for real love.

Although he lived in England, and I didn't see him for the first twelve years after my mother brought us back to Perth to be with her mother in 1964, I managed sporadic visits after that. I did, however, build a wonderful relationship with him, and he was able to spend time with his grandchildren, which gave him great joy before he died in 2002.

I have a sister who is now a lesbian and happily married to her wife of nearly fifteen years, after having several heterosexual relationships with unsuitable men. I'm not sure my brother has ever had a relationship with either sex. Like our father, he is a very private man. I am no longer in contact with either of them. We are truly one very screwed-up family!

Many psychologists have said that if your inner child has been hurt in any way during your formative years, then you are more likely to be attracted to a narcissistic personality. I have done a lot of research about this and see how it is possible. What we lack being given in one area, we make up by providing that in another situation.

It is certainly the case in my life. I collected men who needed a mother figure in some way, and I usually ended up doing everything. I'll put my hand up and admit most of it was because that is what I thought would win them over and make them love me. Let's say I wasn't exactly in the front row when good looks and fine figures were doled out. To offset, I overcompensated by using the assets I had, becoming what they wanted me to be as a woman in their lives. It was like playing a role, over and over again, with some tweaks for their personal wants and needs. Yes, however that played out. They wrote the script; I played the character.

My first marriage ended after having our three children. I went back to working full-time after they had all commenced primary school. I became the soccer mum and taxi while hubby stayed back at work, having a few beers before coming home. GJ believed that if it was good enough for his mother, then that's what I should be doing. And... I accepted that for about ten years. I understand now how my suddenly wanting to change the rules and not always acting the way he was used to would have been confronting for him. We limped on for another five years before separating, then finally divorcing.

My second marriage was short but... not so sweet. We had his teenage children from another partner live with us. They were not used to helping with anything, and that became the fly in the ointment. He wanted a home for his children, as he had had only limited access to them since they were little. Once again, I was attracted to him because he needed someone to look after him. And that's what I did. He helped with the cooking, but the rest of the work was left to me. Unfortunately, he did not instil any boundaries for his children. They did not consider me anything more than someone to be a taxi and keep the house clean and their clothes washed... even if it was a treasure hunt to find them when they were under the bed, on the floor of their bedrooms or, cringeworthy, thrown back into their wardrobes. Anyplace but the washing basket!

When push came to shove, I pushed for him to do something about this situation, and he shoved them and their belongings into a removalist van, along with taking half the house I'd paid for. That's what you call spending your kids' inheritance in a poor financial move!

Is any of this starting to ring some bells with you? Can you see yourself in my shoes, doing what I did or something similar? It is all to curry favour and get the attention you so badly want because your self-love is so low. If I used a wooden mallet to hit the High Striker for Self-Esteem at a carnival, I doubt I'd show anything on the gauge. Hey Ho... for an intelligent woman, I sure knew how to make the silliest of mistakes when it came to choosing a man.

Then there was Arse. As a widower for a couple of years, he did not like living on his own and was out looking for his next victim. He was attracted to me and possibly saw me as another Angel. He needed someone to look after him as he had been conditioned, over the previous thirty-three years, to sit back and be waited on.

I was drawn to his need for love and attention like a moth is to a flame. And we all know how that ends! I was eager to feel needed again after a relationship hiatus. I didn't realise, until it was too late, that I was, once again, being used. And then, after the rape, I stopped doing anything for him, only doing things when I needed to for myself. Can you believe he had the audacity to ask why his washing wasn't done? That's when he upped the ante, and I saw a totally different side to him. No longer was he holding back in his disdain, ably boosted by his mate, Ego. At first, there were subtle digs, especially at my appearance, because I was almost agoraphobic and wouldn't often leave our unit. Then, I was hampered by there being only one car, so I was no longer independent, especially when he was using it much of the time. Little did I know it was often parked in the visitors' car park by the multipurpose area, a place he knew I wouldn't go looking.

How could I not see what was right in front of my face? How could I have been so stupid? How had I gotten myself so far into this situation without realising what it was? He was a narcissist, through and through. The covert passive-aggressive type is the worst type as they are more challenging to identify. I was taken in hook, line and sinker... and he wasn't even an angler.

I'm a very independent and organised woman in both running a household and having a career, yet my soft heart yearned for the impossible dream. Repeatedly I was taken in by stories of the men who saw me as an easy target. I will reiterate, it wasn't always their fault, as I often offered myself willingly... for a chance at love. As I got older and a little wiser, I gained a better insight into what being in a relationship meant. I withdrew from those I thought weren't going to feed my soul the loving and attention it needed and wouldn't give me me the respect I expected and see me as an equal. However, I still made mistakes.

It's a tough gig for men who were born in the 1950s, whose mothers were often stay-at-home ones, at least until the last child started school. Their maternal role model had taught them it was okay not to pitch in and help like their sisters did. For them to be confronted two decades later with 'ban the bra' feminists who believed in equality in everything must have been seen as emasculating and degrading to a large degree. And, although I believed I was a feminist and sang Helen Reddy's song, 'I Am Woman', loudly and proudly, I'm ashamed to say I suffered tremendous guilt when what I really wanted was the dream of marriage and motherhood.

Am I a failure? No, definitely not! Have I made mistakes in choosing men? Yes, on many occasions I have. However, I DID NOT deserve to be raped and then abandoned by Arse as if I was something lower than excrement. It took me three years before I even thought about writing down my experience so that other women and men can look at theirs and make up their minds as to whether they need to address some issues. We are all different, and that must be accepted.

Just because I am now heading down this road doesn't necessarily mean everyone should do the same. It has taken me years of therapy, talking with friends about my trauma, and researching strategies to help me, to some degree, endure the pain and torment I still live with. I doubt anyone can ever feel whole again after a rape and/or narcissistic abuse in a relationship. Still, it is certainly worth the effort to ascend from the depths of despair to find yourself again. In doing so, you will become stronger and rediscover your self-worth and self-love.

WHY AM I ATTRACTED TO BAD BOYS?

Helen Mirren once said this:

> *Before you argue with someone, ask yourself, 'Is that person even mentally mature enough to grasp the concept of a different perspective?' Because if not, there's absolutely no point. Not every argument is worth your energy. ... They're stuck in their perspective, unwilling to consider another viewpoint, and engaging with them only drains you. ... Trying to reason with someone who refuses to see beyond their own beliefs... that's like talking to a brick wall. No matter how much logic or truth you present, they will twist, deflect or dismiss your words, not because you are wrong, but because they're unwilling to see another side. ... Not every person deserves your explanation. Sometimes, the strongest thing you can do is walk away – not because you have nothing to say, but because you recognise that some people aren't ready to listen. And that's not your burden to carry.*
> www.quotefancy.co/helen-mirren-quotes

Chapter 4

The Shit's Hit the Fan

◆◇◆

No woman enters a relationship with bad intentions. She comes in with love, hope and the desire to build something meaningful. But a man's behaviour can shift everything. The way he treats her, respects (or disrespects) her, or nurtures her love or takes it for granted – it shapes the direction of her intentions. A woman who once gave it all can become detached. A once soft and affectionate woman can learn to be distant and indifferent. A woman who once trusted blindly can become someone who questions everything. It's rarely about who she was in the beginning. It's about what she was met with along the way.
www.facebook.com/narcissisticabusesurvivors

Eventually, you hit rock bottom. I'm told you need to go through this process to either seek the help you need or find the strength within to start the fight back. Or, in my case, both simultaneously. The other option is too hard to discuss. It's a very final ending some choose when it gets too difficult to bear any longer. And I can understand that, as I was really close to that at one stage. I had some suicidal thoughts, though I didn't have a plan. It was only the thought of my three children and three grandkids, and how it would severely affect them, that kept me from going down that path. I think eventually learning about the rape was easier on them, emotionally. They still had me in their lives and knew my strength and willingness, as well as the therapy and support I was receiving, would get me through the most challenging times.

I ended up going on a rest and recuperation getaway with Ali, to Hobart. To say Arse was not well-pleased is an understatement, and he tried everything he could to be part of that holiday, even phoning Ali's partner, Mick, to see what he thought about it. He told him, in no uncertain terms, to 'chill out and back off.' This was the same message my second son gave him when he asked to meet up with him and discuss the change in my behaviour. Of course, Arse left out the part that he had raped me. Had Arse told my son why I was withdrawn and not being the dutiful woman of the house, I doubt he would still be free to breathe fresh air instead of sitting bleakly inside a prison cell with its musty odour of sweaty and often unkempt men. So, I had to find my way to the airport, as he refused to drive me, even if I had to wait for a taxi on the side of the road in the dark and cold at three o'clock in the morning.

As I stated in Chapter 1, it was during that time away that I finally confessed what had happened. Ali said it came across as if I was the one who felt guilty. That was how I felt, and I believe it is not uncommon for rape victims to react this way. This was four months after the event. I had held it in, struggled with the toxic pain and torment all that time, while trying to maintain a different face in public.

When I returned home, knowing I would be going to Brisbane again within a month to meet up with Ali and a friend of hers who was a barrister, I was met with the wedding photo of Arse and Angel, pride of place as you walked in the front door. If that wasn't a slap in the face, learning that he had been out on a date with a lady who had recently moved into the village was a punch to the nose. I didn't want anything to do with him, but I believe it is good old-fashioned manners to at least have separation papers filed before you replace the old partner with a new one!

Another thing I learned, much to my chagrin, was that he seemed able to book tickets for flights, the theatre and holiday outings as he was going to visit family in New

South Wales. Normally, he left these things for me to do because he wasn't computer literate. Isn't it amazing how sly and sneaky he was, pretending to be incompetent, just to let me do all of this planning? Yes, I stated it in the last chapter that, being a teacher, I was organised and efficient and became the mother figure, so it was partly my fault too. However, he could have been more assertive, as he was later with his lawyer, and at least offered to learn rather than always expecting me to plan everything. This was another aspect of his narcissistic domination of me. And I was as blind as a bat in not seeing it.

Probably the most hurtful part of this awful spiral I was in was finding out that he was slandering me to anyone in the village who would listen to him. This included those whom he'd just met and who didn't know me personally. Since we had only just moved into the over-55s village two months previously, I was left to do most of the sorting and unpacking. This meant I wasn't a part of his afternoon sessions, drinking and chatting at the garage bar at one of the other units. Therefore, I didn't get to meet many of the other villagers, to the point where one stated he didn't believe I existed!

Due to many finding his defamation of me unacceptable, they complained to the village administration. Thankfully, he was reprimanded. I received a wonderfully supportive letter telling me what had occurred, and I met with the manager. In tears, I told her about the rape, which he had, once again, neglected to tell in his story to the others. She could see the effect it was having. When asked if I had laid charges, I said no. She was another one who pushed me to see my doctor and receive counselling. This was another thing I had neglected to do because of the guilt I felt.

I don't know if anyone, male or female, really understands what you are thinking and feeling unless they have experienced rape and abuse themselves. We should also remember the circumstances of another person's violation are different, and they can only relate it to how they reacted and the place it took them to, physically, mentally and emotionally. Others try to empathise and can be amazingly supportive. However, just like experiencing the death of someone close, the grief you encounter for what has been forcefully taken from you, your dignity, your freedom and your right to safety, especially within what should be a loving relationship, is complicated to deal with for someone close to you.

Eventually, I went alone to my GP, without telling Arse. He was shocked at how I I looked. I was pasty pale because I hadn't been out in the sun, when I usually sported a natural tan for most of the year. Also, I had lost another six kilograms, which is approximately a stone in the imperial measure. The weight on my frame did not suit me. I was like something you could dress in black, hang fake cobwebs from and place in the front window at Halloween.

That was when I learned there would be a conflict of interest, as Arse had also been to see the doctor while I was away, with a sob story about how I was treating him. The lawyer he had engaged was from the same legal firm that the doctor's fiancée worked at. Well played, Arse. I never would have thought you'd know about that, but I'm thinking someone else did and informed you!

I then had to find another doctor at a different practice, even though my lovely GP was one I responded to so well. Once again, Arse had failed to admit his guilt, blaming me for the breakdown in the relationship. My GP willingly referred me to a female colleague, who was gentle and listened while I blubbered my way through my story. It certainly doesn't get any easier the more times you need to repeat it. I was just reliving the trauma of the rape all over again, and my anxiety levels were so high that I constantly felt like vomiting. I was experiencing flashbacks at least several times a week, so I wore anxiety, depression and low self-esteem daily like a veil to cover my face from others. If I'd been in Biblical times, I would have been stoned. If I lived in India now, my family would have killed me for bringing disgrace to them. Knowing this was no excuse for the rape happening in the first place, in what should have been a safe and loving space.

That it happened in my early sixties, long after menopause had passed, which meant that the physical damage internally was significant. Because I didn't receive medical treatment for my tears, when they healed, which seemed to take a long time, I developed keloid scarring, and it has not improved over the years. I have been informed that a new sexual relationship may produce some difficulties! Isn't that just the cherry on the cake? In the meantime, with the aid of the little blue pill, Arse can continue with his relationship that started before the ink had even dried on the court documents. Or was it possibly even earlier, as she was in his dance class? Indeed, there were a few in the village who seemed happy to let me know all about it! Kick a girl while she is down, why don't you!

If it wasn't obvious previously, the fact that he went to dance class by himself, even when I expressed an interest in it as something a couple could do together, speaks volumes. He booked it, yes, all by himself, dressed up to the nines and scurried off to his weekly class. He seemed to leave earlier and come back later as the weeks went by. Apparently, a few of them went out for drinks! And this was pre-rape! She is now down on his Facebook profile as 'In a relationship with…' This I have on good authority, not because I have access to his account, nor would I want to, but because others still like to spread this information as if I want to know. Maybe they are his narcissistic buddies and take great joy in sticking the knife in. Sending me a snapshot of the posting was unwarranted and unwanted. You sometimes wonder if the village is full of idiots. I had deleted and blocked him before the settlement of our separation and financial assets, as my care factor was zero.

All this led me to give up hope that things would get better. I overheard him talking to his mate, Ego, who had obviously asked how things were. Arse's reply, 'She's nothing a bullet wouldn't fix.' At this time, Ego was still sending me texts, trying to pry information out of me by saying, 'If you ever want to talk, I'm here.' I have a copy of a reply that should have gone to Arse, which says, 'She's not giving anything away, Mate.' Conspiracy theory on my part... I think not. The proof is there.

I was also alienated from the wives of our close group of friends. I think this is because they wanted to keep the peace, and they were also under the control of narcissistic men. This group, of course, included Ego. Their silence hurt me immensely, that they didn't ring to see how I was or even want to hear my story. Although I did finally tape a confession from Arse, and he was supposed to have played it to them, I very much doubt that he did. I can't believe other women would not reach out if they knew their friend had been raped by her partner. But I did not receive a call, a text or a message... nothing but silence, which hung like a cold, damp mist in the air around me.

I have said previously that Ego was an extreme, overt narcissist and a very heavy drinker. His dominating personality was overbearing, even when he was sober. Ego's brother-in-law, who was from a European background, sat back while the women did the work. Ego

THE SHIT'S HIT THE FAN

was the same, and as Arse was the only son, he absolutely never had to lift a finger when he lived at home. This was the ideal group for him. And he usually never showed his true self in their presence. If Arse did, it was because Ego had said something cutting in a joking manner. When Arse thought he'd do the same, his filters were unable to hide the true meaning of his words and the barb that was aimed directly at me.

This leads me to how I reacted when I hit rock bottom. Basically, and no other term describes it better, I lived like a hermit. I hid in the second bedroom, generally only coming out when Arse was off at the gym, at water aerobics or playing bowls, something he vowed he'd never do until he realised it was another way to get in with the crowd in the village. Sly as a fox, that one! In our unit, there were two toilets, so I had the one closest to my bedroom. I only used the bathroom, which was the only one available, when he was out, and I locked the doors —one to his bedroom and the other to the passage.

Did I often 'forget' to unlock the bedroom door... maybe, when I was feeling upset over some other thing he had said or done in his true manic, narcissistic style to get a reaction from me. Did I use his toothbrush to scrub my toilet at times or rinse it in the bowl after I had been to the toilet, especially after defecating? You bet I did. Unfortunately, I usually felt remorse and guilt afterwards. It's not in my nature to be vengeful, and I suffered angst because of it.

This added to my descent into the black hole in which I was increasingly finding myself.

I think the most challenging part for me was cutting myself off from socialising with others. I am a gregarious person and love coffee catch-ups, writing and craft groups, going out for lunch or dinner dates with friends and being part of a community. However, I couldn't bear for my friends to see me as I was. I couldn't play the role of carefree Annie for any length of time. It was too taxing on my already very frayed nerves. The community spirit was what I was looking forward to most when I suggested moving into a village complex, but alas, I didn't get to experience it. Arse often put our names down for an event without asking if I'd like to attend. I reluctantly went along. However, after eating very little, I'd hastily excuse myself on the pretext that I needed to get home to my new dachshund puppy. I found it disgusting that Arse would have his arm, proprietary, around the back of my chair and often would sprout endearments while pretending to be the dutiful, loving partner. Instead, he was just Lucifer in disguise.

I've kept the worst till last. As Ali thought, Arse had already commissioned a lawyer. He was also working with both our accountant and the company through which his superfund was managed... and this included my superannuation, which had been rolled over into that account at the 'suggestion' of his accountant. Not my most brilliant financial move and another way to lose more of the kids' inheritance! I never warmed to his accountant, as I believe he was playing with Arse, given his gullibility. Arse thought the accountant was brilliant and did whatever he recommended. Personally, I thought he was pompous and demeaning when he spoke to you… never with you. And, basically, Arse's brief to his lawyer was to get as much of the money out of our combined assets and see me with little or nothing, especially as he knew the state of mind I was in. And he nearly succeeded.

After months of putting up with his narcissistic goading, I made my final offer. He needed to sign the offer then and there, in front of a justice of the peace; otherwise, I would take his taped confession to the police. He offered to drive me to the police station but reneged when I gathered my bag and said, '*Let's go.*' He capitulated and signed. However, being away from the place where the rape and abuse had happened and being able to start a new life four hundred kilometres north meant I was finally able to concentrate on getting myself well again. And I wasn't anywhere where there was a chance I would run into Arse, so he could be out of my life forever.

Unless I finally decide to have him charged with rape. The jury is still out on that… so to speak!

She says she's fine, but she's going insane.

She says she feels good, but she's in lot of pain.

She says it's nothing, but it's really a lot.

She says she's okay, but really she's not.
www.facebook.com/narcissisticabusesurvivors.com

Chapter 5

You've Got This, Girlfriend!

———— ◆◇◆ ————

> *Ignoring someone's needs until they stop asking is not independence, it is neglect. It teaches them their voice doesn't matter, their needs are a burden and their presence is taken for granted. Real love meets needs with consistency, not silence and avoidance.*
> *www.facebook.com/silentwritings*

You've hit rock bottom and now you desperately need to, but more importantly want to, claw your way up from the seemingly endless pit of shit you're floundering in. And you can do it. It will take all your strength. It will take all your courage. It will feel like you're suffocating at times.

It will feel like you're moving forwards, then backwards, especially at the beginning.

These are the stages I went through and the strategies I used. Don't expect everything to change overnight. It takes time, and everyone's timeline is different according to their trauma and their ability to bounce back. It is not a competition. There is no gold medal for who thinks they've pulled through their trauma in the quickest amount of time. I believe you never fully recover from such an ordeal. You may learn to live with it by using some or all of the strategies below, but there will always be at least one piece missing of the jigsaw puzzle that is you.

- **Speak to your doctor:**
  Taking the first step in getting help is often the most difficult because you then have to verbalise what happened. I found it embarrassing. I found it shameful that it happened to me. However, my GP was very supportive and, as well as referring me to a female who specialised in women's health, he wrote up a mental health plan that allowed me five free sessions with a therapist. I was given an appointment with a psychologist. I had two sessions with her; however, I didn't feel we were a good fit. It is extremely important, and I can't stress this enough, that you feel comfortable with and feel listened to by your therapist. If not, find someone else. It's not easy, but it is worth it.

I linked up, by accident, with someone I can only describe as a hippy-style psychologist. She was also into alternative therapies, which I found helpful as I am a big believer in them. Her approach was hands-on, warm and comforting, and the treatment room was like a tent with candles and incense, soft lighting and different types of cosy seating. And she listened. She leaned into me and looked at me when I spoke, often placing a hand on mine when I broke down time and time again. I needed that physical contact. She was also in practice with others who offered Reiki and gong therapy. I had those sessions too. These were my people, but I understand they may not be everyone's cup of tea.

You can get more sessions on a mental health plan, if need be, so don't think five is the limit. Be forceful (if you can) with your GP. It is your right... It's not your fault what happened to you, and no one can say *'I'm fixed'* in five one-hour meetings when suffering from PTSD, depression, anxiety and everything else that is part of it.

- **Join support groups in your local area:**
  This can be done concurrently with getting GP support. These groups can usually be in person or online, and options include, but are not limited to:

- **GROW:** a community-based support for mental health issues, based on mutual support and personal development.

- **Black Dog Institute:** assists greatly with depression and anxiety in different mental health conditions and includes the use of psychoeducational programs.

- **MHFA** (Mental Health Foundation Australia): connects individuals living within an area with similar mental health issues by providing a space for shared experiences and coping strategies.

- **One Door Mental Health:** focuses on mutual support and community connections to various types of groups with specific conditions.

- **SANE:** offers a range of free digital and telehealth support services for those over eighteen years of age. The services are different and what works for you, including counselling, peer support, online groups, 24/7 community forums, online information and resources.

- **Women's Groups:** Some of these are run informally and are under the guise of coffee mornings, yet they provide an opportunity to get out into the community again and make friends. These are often mentioned on Facebook and other social media.

National Helplines and Support Services are also a positive way to receive the immediate help you need. Some people contact them initially and then are guided by them to contact other services such as a GP, a psychologist, or a psychiatrist.

- **Beyond Blue:** a 24/7 telephone service for help with depression and anxiety and to prevent suicide

- **Lifeline:** a 24/7 telephone service for crisis and suicide prevention support for those experiencing emotional distress

- **1800RESPECT:** to support those who have experienced a sexual attack and/or domestic and family violence

- **Re-engage with your closest friends:**
  Be open and honest with them. Many of us cut ourselves off from our greatest support resource because of our perceived shame and guilt. They probably already knew something has happened, even if they didn't know what. They may have also

tried to speak with you about it, but you shut them down by defending him.

They've followed your decline and are waiting to help you when you ask. Allow them to do this. Build up your personal army. It is almost impossible to do it by yourself.

- **Confide in family, if you haven't already done so:** It's not what they are going to want to hear, but they need to support and help you on your journey to recovery. Turn a deaf ear to the naysayers who say, '*I always knew he wasn't good enough*', or '*not in our class*', etc.

    If they are not actively willing to support you, let them go at this time. It serves no purpose having negative people around you while you are rebuilding your self-worth and self-esteem.

- **Choose people who are positive and uplifting:** You need people who are ready to provide practical assistance, such as removing you from the situation by providing accommodation, supporting your AVO/RVO, giving evidence to the police, texting or phoning you daily to make sure you're okay and sending positive affirmations to lift your spirits.

All this goes a long way in ensuring your mindset is focused on the future rather than the past.

- **Last, but by no means least, allow yourself time to breathe:**
  If you haven't already been part of the movement that started many years ago, it's never too late to get on the bandwagon and learn these strategies:

- **Yoga:**
  This practice is essential for enhancing physical health, mental clarity and emotional stability. It offers numerous benefits that promote a healthy and balanced lifestyle. It's not all about 'downward dog' or tying yourself in knots, but rather a gentle way for you to tune in to your mind and body and help nurture and heal it.

  Many see it as stress relief from the constant panic, depression and anxiety they experience that assists them to find a calmness in their turbulent world, particularly after experiencing domestic or family violence, an unwanted sexual encounter or personal threats to their safety.

- **Mindfulness:**
  Regular (daily) practice supports mental clarity, fostering greater well-being and resistance in

everyday life. It helps calm you and resets your mind and body. It can be done anywhere and at any time, which helps to reduce or eliminate panic attacks, feelings of anxiety or depression before they have escalated.

The most popular strategy is employing breathing techniques; others use colouring, games, reading, etc. There are also numerous online mindfulness apps, which are valuable tools.

- **Spiritual healing:**
  It is the practice and experience of restoring, harmonising and balancing our spirit or soul, due to some form of chronic mental, physical and/or emotional wound that needs attention.

> *Spiritual healing occurs as we begin to consciously reconnect with our essential being—the wise, loving, powerful, creative entity that we are at our core.*
> www.azquotes.com, Shakti Gawain, author and teacher

By revealing and soothing the wounds that other modalities, such as psychology, etc., fail to heal, a doorway is opened to a more profound inner spiritual alchemy. In other words, spiritual healing can offer us the chance to grow and transform in a way that no other path can.

The five paths of spiritual healing are physical (the body), emotional (the heart), mental (the mind), spiritual (spirit/soul) or holistic, which includes all of these.

To receive any benefit from this practice, you must go in with an open mind (and heart) and a belief that it will help with your healing.

- **Massage:**
Aahhhhhh... I hear you sigh, just as I do when I think about having one. They assist with reducing anxiety and symptoms of depression and stress, and relieve sleep disturbances, which many people experiencing PTSD, etc., have due to flashbacks or fear of the dark and sleeping, either alone or with someone. It is often thought of as a wonderful cure for migraines.

For many people, a massage is calming, relaxing and pleasurable; however, this is not the case for everyone. If you are a fan, massage is one of the best ways to release your tension and help your body unwind from the way you probably hold yourself most of the time—like a tightly coiled spring, full of raw nerves and ready to jump at any slight movement near you.

My personal favourite is a deep tissue massage. Although it can be painful at times (okay, a lot of the time), it does help soothe the knots in the muscles and help you relax. A day or so afterwards, I love a hot stone massage, to fine-tune my body. Quite often, head and face massages are included. I have learned techniques to target the pressure points on my head and massage these to give me some instant relief when I need it.

Sign up with a TAFE near you, as there are discounted therapies while the students learn the procedures. Or join up and do a massage course yourself, as there are lots of ways you can release the tension stored in your body. That, along with yoga and mindfulness, should help you restore most of your vitality and vigour.

- **Reiki:**
  It may not be for everyone and is probably one method that comes under spiritual healing; however, the benefits far outweigh the scepticism you may have about the practice.

  Reiki reduces stress and can be part of a pain management plan. It also enhances emotional health and regulates body functions, which are often out of kilter in times of upheaval. It assists in anchoring you in the present, along with mindfulness, so you are more focused and have greater clarity. And, naturally, it nurtures spiritual growth through the fostering of personal development.

Personally, I found this very soothing and calming. I didn't need to rehash my story, reopening old wounds I no longer wanted to feel the pain of. The bonus was that I slept very well after each session and awoke refreshed. Weekly visits were my greatest Godsend and worth every dollar.

- **Pet therapy:**
It doesn't matter what pet you have, big or small, mammal, fish or reptile, they all require attention. The repetitive chores help refocus you for a while. If they are the type of pets who like to interact with you, their presence is often the catalyst you need to realise it is not all about you, but there is something relying on you.

My saviour was my dachshund; I think I wouldn't have survived without Sosaj. Having to be responsible for a puppy, to feed him and take him for walks, though this usually happened in the evening or night when the other villagers were not around, meant I had to get up and out of bed even for a short period of time. He walked over the Rainbow Bridge a year ago and my heart shattered.

YOU ARE NOT ALONE

He got me through one of the worst periods of my life, and for that I will be eternally grateful.

I have given you strategies I have tried and tested. Knowing someone was always at the other end of the phone kept my sanity in the early days. As I improved, I moved into employing many of the other techniques. Some I still use regularly today, others not so much. However, I know they are there if or when the Black Dog visits again.

> *You may have experienced a failed relationship. However, the best way to heal your own heart is by focusing on doing the things you love.*
> www.quotesilove.com

Chapter 6

Let's Break It Down

---◆◇◆---

> *It has been said, 'time heals all wounds.' I do not agree. The wounds remain. In time, the mind, protecting its sanity, covers them with scar tissue and the pain lessens. But it is never gone...*
> Rose Fitzgerald Kennedy

What have I said that resonates with others? Through my discussions with some who have experienced the same torment, they say it's like living their lives walking on eggshells, day after day, then as weeks turn into months, they become long, hard years. It's about always being on guard, being wary and not taking chances, and trying to read a situation so it can be defused before the bomb explodes. This is not an easy task and takes its toll. Many have said they feel as if they have lived two lives—their past selves and their current selves.

It's not just the mental and emotional abuse some have had to deal with, but it is also the physical abuse, including sexual exploitation. Many have had years of rape within a relationship. For some of them, fucking rather than making love is all they have ever known. This is so very sad on so many levels. In that way, I have been fortunate. I might have been told to make noises of enjoyment, dress up in lingerie that was way beyond my level of acceptance and talk dirty, but, at least most of the time, I felt relatively safe. However, whether it has happened once or a hundred times, it has still taken from you your pride, dignity and self-worth, and that should never be downplayed.

So, what resonates with you? In Chapter 2, I discussed that, as a personality trait, narcissism can be classed as one of five main types; however, as a mental health condition, there's only one diagnosis... narcissistic personality disorder.

The question is...

- Are you attracted to a **covert narcissist** who is sly in the way they make digs at you, so that you think you are overreacting?
- Or are you taken in by an **overt narcissist**, the life of the party and who appears to be adoring when

you're in public but is the devil in disguise when you're within the four walls of your home?
- This is only magnified even more if you are in a relationship with an **antagonistic narcissist**. True to the meaning of the word, you would instantly pick out this person because they are callous, aggressive and arrogant, and they rarely try to hide it.
- The 'wolf in sheep's clothing' is the **communal narcissist** who present themselves as community-minded and selfless, all the while seeking praise and validation for their charitable works. However, what they are really after is praise and confirmation of their superiority.
- Like cancer, the **malignant narcissist** is deadly with antisocial and harmful behaviours, and you would be in a dictatorial relationship if you were with this narcissistic type.

Whatever your situation, and I can't stress this enough, **it is not about you**. It is about them and their power and control over you. The narcissist mindset can be summed up like this:

> *That didn't happen, and if it did, it wasn't that bad. And if it was, it's not my fault. And if it was, I didn't mean it. And if I did, you made me do it.*
> 'The Narcissist's Prayer' by Dayna Craig

YOU ARE NOT ALONE

If you want to go down the road of charging a narcissist for their behaviour, be it physical, sexual or mental abuse, you have to be sure you can handle the ramifications of it. I am all in favour of seeing justice served. I, however, reacted in a totally different way than what I always stated I would do. I did nothing. In hindsight, would I do that again? No, but at that time I didn't feel I had a choice. I was caught between the proverbial rock and a hard place.

If I did, I would be charging my partner of over five years with rape. I believed we were in a committed and loving relationship. By the time I realised what he was doing, as I outlined in Chapter 4, I was in no fit state mentally to stand up to the public scrutiny that a rape trial would cost me. It wasn't worth putting my family and me through the suffering it would ultimately cause. I had to consider not only how it would affect my children, but also my grandchildren, who, at that time, were too young to understand. And, as far as I'm aware, they are still none the wiser.

If you are in an abusive situation, my suggestion is to start documenting acts of aggression against you. It is never too late to begin, even if the abuse has been going on for what may seem an endless time. Write down the date, time and where the incident took place. Next, record what happened and how you were injured. If you can, take photos. It would also be excellent to note the details of any witnesses. You will have this in case you ever want to make a case against the perpetrator.

Of course, I'd suggest you keep this information somewhere safe, where it is unlikely to be found. This can be quite difficult as many narcissists control everything in the other person's life, including computer access and social media accounts. One person told me she had her file on a USB stick, which was kept in the safe at work. Unfortunately, she has yet to take action, as they are both professional people. I believe, though, things may be about to change.

If you do present to a doctor or hospital with injuries sustained from some form of abuse, ensure you have the doctor note everything down, even if you pretend to have received the injury in another way. They have seen it all before and are probably more aware of what's happening than you are! You need to notarise this as well. The only way for these narcissistic bastards to be found guilty is to have as much evidence as you can about their abuse. It's difficult mentally and emotionally, and you may even feel as if you are doing them an injustice, but that is what they want you to feel and believe. This is how they dominate you, how they wear you down. It is CONTROL, and at your expense.

This is called **coercive control**, which creates, within a domestic relationship, an unequal power dynamic.

Sometimes it is referred to as intimate partner violence. It is definitely a type of emotional abuse that causes psychological trauma, including PTSD and depression. It may also escalate at some stage to include physical abuse. Basically, it is a perpetrator's control through the exertion of a pattern of behaviours. This abuse eventually erodes self-esteem and makes the dependent feel humiliated, intimidated, threatened and fearful. It is a poisonous act, a narcissistic power-play and a brainwashing performance to gain the upper hand in the relationship.

The Australian Institute of Health and Welfare (AIHW) states that 1 in 4 (23% or 2.3 million) women and 1 in 14 (7.3% or 690,000) men, fifteen years and older, experienced physical and/or sexual violence from an intimate partner in 2021-2022. Already statistics being gathered by other sources believe it could be as much as 1 in 3 women experience some kind of domestic abuse, with numbers on the rise. It is definitely thought more men are entrapped by a violent partner, but are too embarrassed to seek help or attention.

Sexual violence is when there is an occurrence, an attempt or a threat of sexual assault which is carried out against the person's will. It may take the form of physical force, intimidation or coercion, and happens when consent is not FREELY given or obtained. This means the person is manipulated into a sexual act against their will. Let call it what it is... RAPE.

Emotional abuse, generally from a narcissistic partner, was at a staggering rate of 25% for women and 15% for men. Rates are actually deemed to be higher than this as many do not confess the brutality they face from their intimate partners due to fear of retaliation, they have no safe place to go and/or there is a lack of financial backing to leave the situation.

These statistics do not include non-physical abuse, as in sexual harassment.

I won't even go into the types of sexual-type activities many women are forced to take part in, but safe to say is it for the enjoyment of the partner alone. The acts are to humiliate, torment, abuse and inflict physical punishment and are despicable in nature, cruel and demeaning. It's not about the act but rather about the power. It's all about the power and the control.

I was only made aware of this during my therapy sessions. As an intelligent woman, I immediately scoffed at being taken in by someone else. Especially a man who had little education and few social skills. If anything, I would have diagnosed him as having ADHD, OCD and possibly a mild intellectual disability. I'm not a psychologist; however, I did teach children with special needs for thirty-five years. Now I know I was deluding myself. I was sucked in by someone who wanted and needed to control someone else to make himself feel better.

What happens in a coercive control relationship? Here are seven points.

- **Monitoring activities:**
    This was a big YES in my case. Arse used his control under the guise of loving me. Although I may have made suggestions about going out to dinner or the movies, he would often decide the activity and whether we would go. And in the end, it came down to what the group of friends, with Ego as the leader, were doing.

    The who, what, why, when and where... if I was to go out alone, needed to be given before I was allowed to go. And I often received mobile calls from him during that time. It was best to answer those...

- **Exerting financial control:**
    You all know I fell into the proverbial trap here. So, another YES. Although my brain yelled *no, no, no*, the accountant and Arse demanded *yes, yes, yes*, for me to roll over my super into his self-managed fund. And, like I fool, I was Pooh Bear to a honey pot.

    Arse was regularly checking our bank account and often questioned my expenditure. As an independent person, I had not come across this previously. Arse did, however, let me pay the bills online, even though he was perfectly capable. I now view this as him allowing me some control, even though he had motives behind it.

- **Isolating the other person:**
  I'm really doing well in my scores here... YES, again. By always wanting to come with me when I was seeing friends, many with whom I had long associations, my invitations gradually dwindled unless I went out while he was at the gym, bowls or water aerobics. And, he would have preferred I go to those with him, too.

  Family activities were also limited, especially with most of my family four hundred kilometres away. I'm sure the three kids met up together, not inviting us, as they didn't want Arse around.

- **Insulting the other person:**
  This was very subtle. But it happened, and it became more prominent over time. Another YES. Woo hoo— four out of four! Arse constantly commented on my weight, what comfort food I ate, why I should do more exercise... the list goes on.

  In the end, I paid $25,000 of my money to have gastric sleeve surgery. If that wasn't coercion, I don't know what was!

- **Making threats and being intimidating:**
The perpetrator uses this to scare and torment his victim. That's what you call 'upping the ante.' Even before the rape, Arse had started to niggle me. It was about small, insignificant things at first but later escalated to the point where I couldn't handle what he was saying or doing.

Three incidents stand out as being particularly intense. During a drive home from an outing, after leaving early because I had a migraine, he wasn't happy. He let me know this, over and over again. You can imagine how wound up I was getting. Eventually, I told him to *'Shut the fuck up.'* His reply... *'I'm going to drive off the road and into a tree.'* I would be the one killed. After that, there was silence. He had kicked the winning goal and, if his smirk was anything to go by, he knew it.

Another time, again while he was driving, he was being particularly obnoxious and pushing all my buttons. I was feeling very nauseous, another migraine brewing, and asked him to stop. He didn't. I probably asked about another five times, getting louder and louder, before he complied. He didn't say anything but kept on driving until I was gagging. When he stopped, he acted as the loving partner because there were people around and waved off any help from others. Again, a winning try for him.

After the rape, he made physical threats to me all the time. He held up his fist as if to punch me and called me unspeakable names. Arse goaded me. I had little patience and ended up screeching like a banshee. Not my proudest moment, but it was all I had left in my empty tank.

That's a fifth YES.

- **Using sexual coercion:**
I now know I was also raped one of the first times I was with Arse at his place, the night he made me dinner. We were kissing, as a new couple does, before he pushed me back on the lounge. I was pinned down by his weight and strength, and he removed my knickers and plunged his fingers into my vagina, before taking off his shorts and entering me. Once again, it was mercifully short.

Although it caused no real pain, I wasn't expecting it, nor would I have agreed to it so early in the relationship. Sex was often like that between us. It usually happened when he wanted it, and there was only minimal foreplay. It is, apparently, how he and Angel made love. I think it was just sex, rather than love, myself. In order to keep me satisfied, and this is where the coercion comes in, he did have moments when the romantic in him came out and he made sure I was sexually satisfied.

Smart move, Arse. Another YES—you're playing like a champ.

- **Involving children or pets:**
Even though Angel had grandchildren, they never stayed over. I believe this is because Arse wouldn't have liked it. I always had my grandies stay, so I pushed for this to continue. He had no clue how to interact with them, and I had to remind him often, if they said no to tickles or being touched when they were playing, he needed to listen to them. This led to us having 'discussions' about children's rights, which he thought were ridiculous. This was an ongoing battle for me and had me very tense whenever they stayed.

After the rape, I bought a dachshund puppy. I needed him to keep me sane. We also had another dog, which Arse claimed as his own. My pup was often on my lap when I was watching TV in the lounge, usually because Arse was out socialising. When he came home, he made a point of going to pat him, especially after the time I shouted in desperation, *'Don't touch him!'* He knew how to torment me. The final straw was that he thought he should keep my pup as well when I left, as his dog would be bereft without him. I doubt he was serious, but he knew it upset me, and that was his aim.

LET'S BREAK IT DOWN

One hundred per cent I scored. Again, nothing to celebrate. It was a persistently numbing relationship, which, over time, left me drained, unsure of myself and feeling incompetent in dealing with most everyday tasks. I was the fly in his spiderweb, and, at that time, I saw no way to escape.

> *Your new life is going to cost you your old one. It's going to cost you your comfort zone and your sense of direction. It's going to cost you relationships and friends. It's going to cost you being liked and understood. But, it doesn't matter. The people who are meant for you are going to meet you on the other side, and you're going to build a new comfort zone around the things that actually move you forward. Instead of liked, you are going to be loved. Instead of understood, you're going to be seen. All you're going to lose is what was built for a person you no longer are. LET IT GO.*
> Brianna Wiest

Chapter 7

I'M Screwed Up...
BIG TIME

---◆◇◆---

She laughs with everyone... But breaks when no one's looking. She's called strong like it's a compliment, but no one sees the weight she carries in silence. How she shows up for everyone else while quietly falling apart inside. She's not asking for much. Someone to notice that she's tired too. She keeps going.

Not because she's okay. But because she's learned not to expect much from anyone anymore. And it hurts less that way.
www.facebook.com/Fifty Shades of Tired

YOU ARE NOT ALONE

At some point, you will start to realise you are not the same as you used to be. You may find, as I did, that you are becoming withdrawn and not interested in what you used to love. Reading and writing were my two greatest passions. However, I found it difficult to summon up the enthusiasm to pick up a romance book, one of my favourite genres, and immerse myself in the fairytale of the love that unfolded between the pages. And, with the romance killed in my relationship by the rape, I felt no compulsion to write about it either. I stopped journalling as well. That was probably one of the worst things I could have done. Writing down my feelings and my thoughts may have made me face the actions of Arse earlier and therefore seek the assistance and the therapy I needed sooner than I did.

I found that what I tolerated previously, I no longer did. My patience had started to be worn thin, even before the rape. However, I hadn't put two and two together to reach the conclusion that Arse was a narcissistic bastard. Once I did, instead of remaining quiet, I spoke the truth. This just fuelled his fire. Arse is a typical Leo, and I was poking the lion with a stick. In hindsight, not the wisest move to make on the chessboard of our relationship. I was understanding the value of my voice and realised that he no longer deserved my focus, my energy or my time. I was ready to walk away, this time on my terms.

As Karla Grimes stated on www.narcissisthunters.com,

I'M SCREWED UP... BIG TIME

> *'A narcissist paints a picture of themselves as being the victim or innocent in all aspects. They will be offended by the truth. But what is done in the dark will come to light. Time has a way of showing people's true colours.'*

This is what was happening in the relationship between Arse and me. I gave a few examples in the previous chapter as to how he had started to press my buttons, even before the rape. As a Libra, I like things in my life to be balanced, and he was definitely rocking my scales, big time!

I was told something very profound when I was at rock bottom. I was still considering the option of leaving all the pain and shame behind me and just slipping away to another world where peace reigned. It's as final as it gets. Then I was told I wasn't broken. I was badly dented, that was a definite. I was chipped and scratched in the battle, again true. I was crinkled and rumpled and, to be truthful, in need of a good iron. And I certainly was torn, in more ways than one.

Take a moment to think about this. Imagine two $100 notes. One is in pristine condition and worth every cent. The other has been in circulation for many years and has seen better days. Tell me... which note has the greatest value? Neither does. They are of equal value, each worth $100. I am worthy, you are worthy, whether we are in immaculate condition or soiled in some way. This is a mantra we need to keep telling ourselves—*I am worthy, I am strong, and I am focused on finding myself again* (Annie Chandler, 2023).

How would you view yourself after what has happened to you? We all see things differently, and it depends on many things, though mainly our upbringing. If it was a stringently religious one, you may reject religion altogether once you can. If there was domestic violence present in the home in which you grew up, statistics say you are likely to seek out that type of relationship, even though you loathed it when you were younger. If there was sexual abuse, then you are predisposed to accepting that within your relationships.

It is called conditioning, which is really a type of grooming. To you, it becomes the norm in your relationships, and you don't believe that you are worthy of anything better. It is sad, and it is NOT true. You are worthy of being treated as a human being, who is able to receive love and live in a safe environment.

Another way to view yourself is as a building. Whether it be a house, a shop or a warehouse, there is value in property. Think about the old saying, *'Buying the "Worst" House on the "Best" Street is a Smart Decision.'* (www.ithinkproperty.com.au) This is because you instantly have equity value in it, as well as controlling the value you can add through renovations and upgrades. The main point here, however, is that any building you buy, unless you are going to demolish it and start again, must have a solid foundation. And we all know what, with reference to people, 'demolishing' means. It is, once again, that final step some choose when their trauma is too hard to carry any longer.

So, let's assume we want to invest in the 'worst' property... that is what I did, and I'm hoping that is your choice as well. Our foundations are strong, we have a pretty good skeleton and although the roof may not be all there, it can be fixed. What's the first thing we need to do? Good question. At the time I was at my worst, my synapses were not snapping terribly well, and a lot of what people said or tried to communicate to me was lost. I had a very leaky roof. Therefore, I called in the experts, the roof restorers, to help me. Therapy, as in a one-on-one situation, was brilliant. I'm not sure I made much sense in the beginning, as I jumped from one story to another, but the psychologists had heard it all before and could join the dots I was unable to.

Think about this statement from Shahida Arabi on www.narcissisthunters.com and how it relates to you. I know you are important, and your healing is paramount.

> *'Healing from narcissistic abuse is a journey, but one that is worthy of taking. It starts with acknowledging your pain and taking steps towards self-care and self-love.'*

Therapy saved my life. Therapy changed my life. Therapy mended my roof and made it functional again. Or, as my children 'lovingly' said, it (my brain) is the best it will be at my age! Am I worth more now I've fought my demons and generally won the contest? I believe I am. The fact was that not only did I have to contend with Arse the narcissist, but I also needed to reach my inner child and patch the cracks that were apparent in my foundations. This was the only way I could successfully move on, and I hope you realise the importance of this step in your own recovery.

Looking in the mirror to really see what stares back at you can be daunting, even for the bravest of us. When you are battle-sore and weary, it takes an even greater effort. Why do it? My simple answer is... If you don't, you are only hiding from yourself. And that does not make the issue go away. In fact, it magnifies it.

Another way to view this is thinking you are an onion. Looking back through your life is like peeling an onion. There are many layers. If the inner layer has some rot, then you can be fairly confident it has also infected the whole vegetable to some degree. It is what I had to address, and I'd lay a bet with poor odds that it is what you will have to do as well. It is intimidating, but you can't conceal what is in front of you. It must be tackled if you are to heal and move forward.

There is no easy way to do this, however. I know this is not what you want to hear, but it is necessary. As I stated previously, it is like having to rip off a band-aid that is stuck to the wound scab. You want to go slowly, knowing how painful it will be. However, that is not a good idea. It is a big mistake. Take a deep breath, and breathe out as you rip away as quickly as possible. You know it will probably bleed again, and that is expected. A deep wound is like the old Pantene advert; It (the healing) won't happen overnight, but it will happen.

Given time and support, the pain will gradually lessen. You should also start to 'find' yourself again and, hopefully, go back to the activities you enjoyed pre-trauma. Eventually, the wound will disappear. You will, however, have a scar. My advice is to wear that as a badge of honour. It should be a reminder of how far you have come and what you have achieved. What you have gone through was horrendous. We each have our stories, and, as I will say again, they cannot be compared. No tale is worse than another. We have been crippled by the atrocities we've had to endure as a result of being with a narcissist. Our lives will never be the same, but we don't have to let them win by giving up.

Seek help. It is out there. I have listed some avenues open to you in Chapter 5. All it takes is that first step. It is always the hardest, but well worth the climb to the top. If you need to pause and draw breath at any time, that's your prerogative. If you feel you have to go back a few steps while you adjust to the change in altitude, that's okay too. It is your journey. Your path will not be the same as mine.

I travelled all over the place in my quest to find myself again. I'm not great with directions at the best of times, even with Google Maps, so my journey was up hill and down dale. I had to wade through streams that were often too deep, only to be met with a rocky cliff face. I'm afraid of heights. Dying seemed a better option at that time. However, I had a support crew who harnessed me up and held the ropes taut at the bottom as I found footholds to lever myself up. It was an extremely slow process and the hardest of all the tests I endured. The fact that I made it gave me hope for the future.

Every day since then, I'm grateful for how far I've come. And I am mindful to express my gratitude to the Universe daily. Life may never be the same, but from where I'm standing at the moment, it's fucking fantastic!

Your role, should you intend to accept it, is to help someone else from the quagmire of their traumatic life. We can all help each other. You don't have to write a book and go on a speaking circuit. Just be open to the needs of others during their bleakest times. Listen to their stories and try not to make it about yours. Actively listen. Hear what they are saying, what they are asking, and give no more, no less. We are all children of this Universe and have a right to peace, to love and be loved and to be respected.

As a survivor of narcissistic abuse, I have felt the pain, both physically and mentally, of the trauma inflicted upon me. I've also realised I have the strength and resilience that comes with healing and reclaiming the power that had been taken from me. I'm continuing my fight. If I can, hopefully, so can you.

This is why I encourage you not only to seek therapy, but to reach out to others who have a similar story. As one, we are vulnerable. As a group, we wield more power. However, as an army, we can be indestructible.

If you go down the route of charging your partner with physical, sexual and/or emotional abuse, having a crowd with you in the courtroom is powerful. *'All for one, one for all'* is more widely known as the catchphrase for The Three Musketeers. It does, however, originate in Shakesphere's *The Rape of Lucrece*. The meaning behind it shows a strong sense of solidarity, collective unity and mutual support. This is the least we can do for another human being who is wearily treading a path yet not knowing which direction to take. Be a leader and take them home.

I don't want your apology. I want you to feel what I felt when you broke me. I want the weight of your actions to sit with you in silence, just like I sat with all the pain you left behind. One day, I hope it hits you that you lost someone who truly cared. And when it does, I hope it hurts. Not because I want to see you suffer, but because I want you to finally understand what it feels like to be destroyed by the person you trusted most.
www.facebook.com/Fifty Shades of Tired

Chapter 8

I'm So Pretty, Oh So Pretty... NOT

---◆◇◆---

Relationships With Narcissists Are Permeated by Loss
- ❖ *You lose yourself.*
- ❖ *You lose your self-respect and dignity.*
- ❖ *You lose your self-esteem.*
- ❖ *You lose your sense of reality.*
- ❖ *You lose your ability to function well.*
- ❖ *In many instances, you lose your financial resources.*
- ❖ *You may lose your mental and physical health.*
- ❖ *You lose your friends and family.*
- ❖ *You lose your innocence.*

> ❖ *You lose your feelings of safety.*
> ❖ *You lose your trust.*
> ❖ *You lose your sense of well-being.*
> ❖ *You lose your faith in people, life and sometimes even God.*
> ❖ *You lose your hopes and your dreams.*
> ❖ *You may lose your assets.*
> ❖ *You may even lose your desire to live.*
> *And there is so much more...*
> *This is the one thing in life that has the potential to destroy everything.*
> Maria Consiglio @understandingthenarc

The Loss of Self

Metaphorically speaking, I didn't want to be attractive anymore. I certainly didn't want attention. Hiding away was my option, from myself as well as others. I felt ugly, as if I was wearing some band on my forehead that said I was not pure, I was unworthy of love and I should be condemned for what I believed were my sins... A modern-day Mary Magdalene.

I believe the writing above by Maria Consiglio perfectly sums up what many of us lose at the hands of a narcissist. I could tick every one of those points, some holding precedence over others. At the top of my list would be the loss of feeling safe, especially since I continued to live in the small three-bedroom unit Arse and I had moved into just months before the rape. My lawyer suggested it was the best option, IF I could handle it. Arse was already having his lawyers hold off from replying to mine, hoping I would cave in and leave. So many nights I lay awake, wondering how much longer I could last, confined to my bedroom. It was like a prison cell. If I left, I risked losing my financial resources and assets. In the end, I signed over 70% to Arse. My need for freedom was greater than my need for material wealth.

This is a part of the trauma cycle. You blame yourself for what happened to you. You take responsibility for someone else's actions. My self-esteem plummeted like shares on the stock market, along with all sense of self-respect and dignity. Why? Because this had been happening for a long time. Arse had been chipping away, seemingly quite innocently, though I now know it was intentional.

The more he didn't say 'thank you' or give compliments, the harder I worked, hoping for a positive response from him. I even modelled what to say or do, as I did with my students. I thought he was unaware that he was neglectful in this way. Now I know differently. This is aptly summed up in this quote from MentalHealth.com:

> 'Narcissism... is a psychological condition characterised by an excessive need for admiration, a fragile sense of self-worth, and difficulties forming genuine emotional connections. While admiration and love are fundamental human desires, narcissists often struggle to differentiate between them, favouring admiration as it offers a sense of control and validation that love does not.'

To me, truer words were never spoken. What do you think?

I certainly didn't function well. Communication was difficult, especially with my family and friends before they knew what had happened to me. I didn't realise how badly a decline in both emotional and physical health can affect that. And I pushed them away, declined offers to meet up, made excuses and generally stopped taking calls and reading text messages. In the end, many but a few stopped trying to get a response from me.

If my communications were poor, my memory was even worse. All sense of reality flew out the window. Days went into weeks. Without appointments sent to my phone by my psychiatrist, which she made me accept before I left the room, I doubt I would have remembered. I no longer ran by a schedule, nor did I look at a calendar, which were things I did on a daily basis as a teacher, and as a person who anally organised her life.

Can you relate to any of this in your situation?

The Mask of Shame

Being a child of parents who lived apart, in two different countries, across the world from each other, my trust in adult role models was damaged at an early age. Then there were twelve years of being at the mercy of nuns, many of whom didn't practice what the bible preached. Next was the platter of young adult males saying, 'I love you' but really meaning 'I want to get into your knickers.'

Oh, where did my innocence go? Or did I ever really have it? Probably not, looking back over the sixty years of my life I can recall. However, being raped by someone who is supposed to love you and be committed to you means the end of many of your hopes and expectations, dreams and desires. That's when there were fleeting moments when the pain was unbearable and an endless sleep seemed a better option. Thankfully, something always pulled me back from the brink.

My faith was tested in many ways. Faith in myself, that I would make the correct decision and faith in others that they would be there when I was ready to tell them what happened. I was raised a Christian; however, lately, I have looked towards more spiritual guidance through a sisterhood group. Here, I feel I have finally found my tribe, my sisters, my niche. It has given me purpose again and a reason to rise up with strength and passion to help others walking the road I am on. This quote from Buddha spoke to me:

> 'When it hurts to move on, just remember the pain you felt hanging on.'

I hope it resonates with you, as well.

Literally, I couldn't look at the gaunt figure I'd become. It made no difference to me what people thought of me when they saw me like that. In Chapter 1, I outlined how my general health and hygiene were questionable at the best of times and awful at the worst. Apparently, I'm not the only rape victim to lose their need to keep themselves clean as they usually did. You feel dirty, so you become dirty in many ways.

It certainly didn't help that Arse had an indecent love of men's magazines, the 'under-the-counter' type. He even had one of those calendars, with skimpily dressed, big-breasted women lying prostrate over race cars, farm machinery and motorbikes. He was indignant when I asked him to look at them in private, as it wasn't something I would want my young grandchildren to inadvertently find. Not to mention that I believe they denigrated women. Don't let me start on the porn sites. He seemed to have a fetish for grandmas being with younger men. I'm wondering if that was because Angel was a dozen years his senior, had a grown family who had all flown the proverbial nest, and, in his words, 'was a great root.' Like I needed to know that!

Therapy as Reset

So, what changed this for me? I'll keep repeating it, ad infinitum, THERAPY. Before you can move on, you need help. Your brain is telling you you're the one at fault. The narcissist is reinforcing this because he knows you've temporarily lost the battle. Your thought patterns need to be reset. It's like winning Monopoly's 'Get Out of Jail Free' card. You have a chance to reclaim parts of your old life you so desperately need in order to function as a human being again. Once you are on the way to doing this, and you are becoming stronger, you start to question things that happened and why they happened. Hopefully, you will see that you were coaxed and coached to do as the narcissist wanted. You were a marionette, with him skilfully pulling the strings to make you do his will. It's brainwashing, particularly if he is a covert narcissist, as Arse is.

> *'The only person you can control is yourself. Stop trying to change or control the abuser.'*
> Melody Beattie, www.mindingtherapy.com

Setting Boundaries

There's something magical about reaching the point where you're ready to set a limit, to set boundaries. When we believe what we say, others will take us seriously, too. Things will change, not because we're controlling others but because we've changed. We have found a way to regain control so that they no longer have the power. The ball is back in our court. It's all about resetting the way we think, feel and act. Sometimes we have to put on a mask and 'fake it till you make it.' This idea comes from Simon and Garfunkel's single 'Fakin' It,' released in 1968. I'm pretty sure most of us have done this at some time during our lifetime—as an employee or a new parent, at an interview or performing in front of others.

The message here is to persevere. Having an optimistic mindset is the first step. Taking control of your fears and working your way through them allows for much-needed healing. It takes courage, lots of it. It's also about having the tenacity to keep going, even when the road becomes steep and narrow and the weather is wet and windy.

I'M SO PRETTY, OH SO PRETTY… NOT

Know your enemy. They are showing their hard outer shells at this time, but remember, there is often a softer underbelly you can aim for until you have the strength to face them head-on. Knowledge is a powerful source; finding out everything you can about narcissism will ensure you are informed as to likely scenarios. Miguel de Cervantes said, '*Forewarned is forearmed*'. We should heed this message.

Recovery is not cheap, mentally or physically. It can also hit the back pocket, too, if you need to pay for extra therapy sessions, as I did. These were not covered by my private healthcare provider. Funny that there's nothing in their list of services that says, 'extra therapy after rape'! If there were, how many of us would think we would need to tick that box? I certainly wouldn't have.

I thought I was in a good relationship. When I was searching through online dating sites after the demise of my second marriage, and after a break from being in a relationship, I seemed to be drawn to widowers. I believe this was because, in my eyes, they had passed the test of time, and it was the death of the spouse that ended the relationship, rather than the drama of divorce. I'm sure it is still a very good argument, just not in Arse's case… as I found out.

On the tape I have of his confession, and during another conversation as well, he mentioned that he also raped Angel, again while he was supposedly asleep. Several friends, including males, have questioned, 'How could he not know he was raping you? He couldn't possibly have done it in his sleep.' That never occurred to me, probably because he repeatedly said, 'It doesn't count; I was asleep.' The fact that he knows he did it to Angel must mean she said something to him. I believe he knew he was wrong on both counts and just didn't want to admit it, more to himself than anyone else.

I like this quote:

> 'You will never see how toxic someone is until you breathe fresher air.' (Unknown, www.scarymommy.com/narcissist-quotes)

Now I have managed to escape, colours look so much brighter, the sun shines even when it rains and there is hope for the future.

> ***How to Get Over a Narcissist***
> 1. *Go no contact*
> 2. *Anticipate potential manipulation*
> 3. *Try to reconnect with old hobbies or passions*
> 4. *Write down your reasons for ending the relationship*

I'M SO PRETTY, OH SO PRETTY... NOT

5. Surround yourself with the right support
6. Ensure you have the right lawyer
7. Store belongings or momentos
8. Be mindful of tendencies to rationalise
9. Try to build more self-love and self-kindness
10. Allow yourself to grieve
11. Be mindful of moving on too quickly
12. Join a support group
13. Stay connected with online support

www.choosingtherapy.com

Chapter 9

Vomit Out the Hate – It's Cathartic

―――――――◆◇◆―――――――

You finally opened up about something real. Maybe you've finally talked about your struggles with your family, that thing you're excited about but scared to pursue, or why you've been quiet lately. Now you're lying awake, dissecting every word you said.

Was that pause too long? Did you overshare? Why did you mention that detail? You're checking their texts for signs they're pulling away, analysing if they seem uncomfortable, convinced you've revealed too much and ruined everything. The vulnerability

> *felt right in the moment, but now it feels like you're walking around emotionally naked.*
>
> *Why does your brain do this? Brené Brown coined 'vulnerability hangover' for good reason; it's that emotional exposure hangover after we've shown up authentically. Your brain is essentially running a threat assessment on emotional risk.*
>
> *Studies show our brains process social rejection in the same regions that process physical pain, so after being vulnerable, your mind scrambles to predict and prevent potential rejection. It's reviewing the footage, looking for danger signs, trying to protect you from the possibility that your realness might push people away.*
> www.Dailywellness.com, 14 August 2025

When I finally spoke of the rape in April 2022, four months after it happened, it felt as if a secret I was finding difficult to keep was allowed to be shared. That feeling of letting go lasted about a day. Then I fell back into a hole again. A deeper hole, if that were possible. It meant I would have to accept that things were changing, and I would have to decide what stance I would take. I had spent a wonderful week with my sister, enjoying my freedom, but realised

I was to fly back to how I had been living, hidden away. And I knew it was time to make some important decisions. These would be very important decisions that would not only impact me, but also my family.

However, once 'home' again, my resolve slipped... a lot. My sister had again arranged for me to meet with her, where she was living in Brisbane, and I had an appointment with a barrister friend of hers. His advice echoed hers... engage a lawyer, the sooner the better. Even though he was unable to represent me, he did, however, look through our finances, make notes and offer much-needed advice. I was thankful for anything at that stage. My cognitive ability was poor, much like someone who had suffered a stroke and was trying to piece together their life.

By that time, I was fortunate enough to have some sessions with my 'alternative' therapist. Part of the healing process was to forgive Arse so that I could move forward in my recovery. I found this almost impossible but summoned the courage and did as was suggested. To say I was underwhelmed by his response is an understatement. Having to hold his hands and try to look him in the eye was nearly impossible, but saying the words, 'I forgive you for everything you have done to me' had me almost gagging.

I'm not sure what outcome I expected. It certainly wasn't his response, something along the lines of 'as you should be.' He was still steaming at the three-page typed letter I had left on his desk in response to his earlier nasty note to me, before I went to Brisbane. He had, of course, given it to Ego to read. Ego very firmly stated his opinions, which quickly became Arse's. And, of course, they were not as I specifically wrote them.

Mathew Martorana is an American motivational speaker who often writes about narcissists on his Facebook page. In one post, he states,

> *'To get rid of a narcissist, you first need to understand their game: they either seek praise or provoke you. If you're not feeding their ego, they'll stir up some drama just to feel in control over you. They enjoy your anger as much as your admiration.'*

How apt is this? It's also a pity I didn't know about narcissism until after the rape. It may have saved me a lot of angst and helped me to be prepared for some of the shit that was to follow.

My life then revolved around visits to my lawyer, a wonderful man who practised family law and was so understanding. I still tended to cry a lot whenever I had to go through what happened, and I'm positive I wasn't answering many of the questions he asked. Fortunately, he always emailed me the information he required to support my case, since I would have forgotten what was needed. It was also fortunate that I was a very good record keeper and had a filing cabinet of accounts, household purchases and joint bank account details, including where my super was rolled into and the investments we held. I scanned and emailed anything I thought would be applicable.

Arse, on the other hand, had no idea where this information was. I am sure, however, that he did get Ego's brother-in-law, who was a techie, to go through my computer while I was away. Arse would have known my pin code, as it was the same for everything, and I thought I could trust him. There was a rebooting, etc, that was required when I first logged in, so I changed my password very quickly on everything I could think of.

There were also regular doctor visits. After realising I needed to change doctors as Arse and I had the same one (even though the GP had been mine originally), I needed to go through everything once more with the female doctor. She was lovely, listened intently and was concerned by what had happened, especially at my age. She also did a vaginal inspection. It was over twenty years since I'd needed a pap smear, and longer since my hysterectomy, so it was daunting. And frightening. And uncomfortable. What she saw was some redness and raised scar tissue, what she expected after a rape when the internal tearing hadn't been medically treated.

Let's not forget the therapy sessions with a couple of different psychologists. They were good, but I found opening up immensely challenging. One was quite young, probably in her thirties... maybe. I wondered what life experiences she had, or whether it was all textbook knowledge. The way she spoke, I believe it was the latter. The group sessions were easier as there were others in the same boat. Not necessarily raped, but having been in domestic violence situations or having sex used as a weapon. This was a whole new world for this sixty-plus-year-old who thought she was wise to the ways of the world. Apparently, I'd lived in a bubble all my life. Or pretended, more likely, that I was living my dream. How wrong I was.

Besides speaking with my children, reconnecting with some of my closest friends was tough. I felt embarrassed, ashamed and vulnerable. Although, as an educated woman, you know it wasn't your fault, the little child inside is cringing and hiding from what happened. When you have completed as many courses as I now have on the inner child, narcissism, domestic violence and the like, you build up a tougher shell to protect yourself. This is when I reached out to others. They were amazing, and most had their own stories of visits from the black dog, domestic and sexual abuse, or feelings of inadequacy and being overwhelmed by even the smallest things. We had each been trying to be brave on the outside, while often a total mess internally. This made a special bond on another level. As the saying goes, a problem shared is a problem halved.

VOMIT OUT THE HATE – IT'S CATHARTIC

Where did I go from there? I had always been a fan of writing down thoughts and feelings, not necessarily daily (diarising), but certainly after an event, either joyful, like the weddings of my sons, or sorrowful, as in the break-up of a relationship. From this, I followed the trend of journalling. It's *'same, same, but different,'* as goes the Thai tourist catchphrase. Once again, I'd make an entry whenever I felt the need. Sometimes it would be a goal I wanted to achieve, along with the process I'd follow to achieve it. Sometimes I'd write about my life, my family and their achievements. This time, I'd embellish it with affirmations, stickers or photos I'd sourced on the internet. I tried to keep this journal uplifting in content so I could revisit it whenever I needed a boost.

I gave this up after the rape and didn't return to it until I was in therapy. Initially, it was testing both my ability to think and vocalise what I felt. It felt external to me, as if I had to write it in a foreign language. Keep at it, if you are going to go down this path, as the benefits, in the long run, by far outweigh the challenges. I am at the stage where I can now reread some of my entries. There are those that are dark, and it still frightens me to see where I was. It is also wonderful to ride the wave as my mental state improved, and I began to see a rainbow breaking through the clouds, knowing that the sun was shining somewhere.

Another gem I found very helpful, and yes, I am quite alternative, is seeking affirmations that reflect what I need to hear. I'd write them out and stick them on the fridge, on the bathroom mirror, in fact, anywhere I would see them regularly. I'd change them as needed. I found the best thing is to actually speak them out loud. Speak with confidence and, if you can, look into a mirror as you say the words. Apparently, if you hear and speak the affirmation, it has a greater effect. Please, please, please… believe what you are saying for success.

One pearl of wisdom from a therapist was to disassociate myself from anyone and anything that recalled unpleasant feelings and emotions, caused me stress and angst and had me living flashbacks. At the beginning, I felt I was going nowhere. It's probably the same with many others. It's about waking up, getting up and putting one foot in front of the other until we find our resilience and resolve to move forward. It's cathartic. I sold the jewellery that Arse had bought me and eventually either gave away or sold anything I brought up from Perth when I moved north. There is nothing in my home now that has any connection to him. Delete photos from your phone, tablet and computer, as well as delete and block people with whom you no longer wish to associate. That was your old life. In order to start afresh, you must first purge. It's like a detox. Your system needs to be cleansed. It's amazing how much better you will feel, as I did and continue to do.

I also stopped going to restaurants, cafés and other places we would go to as a couple, or in the group with which we associated. I have not visited the shopping centres near where we lived and rarely go to that area, unless meeting up with friends. When I moved, I once again changed my GP and only divulged the rape as I was still having problems in my vaginal region. Of course, I changed my dentist as the receptionist was the daughter of a friend of Arse's, and definitely the accountant, whom I disliked from the very first meeting! It was easy to do as it tied up that part of my life very neatly, so, metaphorically speaking, it could be placed in the bin for rubbish collection day.

My last suggestion is tongue-in-cheek. Get a dart board and put your perpetrator's face on it... if you need to go that far. I don't condone violence, even if it is pretend. However, sometimes, you need to let off some steam. This is a much safer option than others have taken in hunting down the other person and actually wounding or murdering them, no matter the atrocities they caused. They need to be the ones rotting in the jail cell, not you.

These are steps I took and ones I found worked in my recovery. After the rape, I was mentally and physically wrecked with no idea how I was going to mend. Or even if I was able to mend. Fortunately, I had people around me, my family and friends, my therapist and groups, with whom I could bare my soul and feel supported. It was pretty grim where I went in my mind at times, and it's still unpleasant to look back four years later. Time does heal some things, but you may feel scared for the rest of your life and have the scars to prove it.

There will be days when you have to admit that you are not okay and haven't been for a long time. And you cry it out for as long as you need to. There's nothing wrong with that.
Stephanie Bennett-Henry, www.Bing.com/images/, '50 Quotes: It's Okay Not to be Okay'

Chapter 10

I'm on My Way to Loving Life Again

---◆◇◆---

> *You are not responsible for the abuse inflicted upon you. You are not responsible for the choices that the abuser makes. But you are responsible for your own healing.*
> Christine Hammond, www.narcissisthunters.com

As a survivor of narcissistic abuse, I know firsthand how the trauma and ongoing pain drain you of everything you are. However, I also know that my renewed strength and resilience came from my healing. I was able to then reclaim my power and eventually move forward.

On www.abusewarrior.com, I found a quote that helped me take my initial steps. It was given to me by my psychologist in the early days.

> *'There is no safe way to remain in a relationship with a person who has no conscience. The only solution is to escape.'*

This was one of my first mantras, which I wrote down and kept with me always as a reminder of what I needed to do. It is amazing that this popped up again on my Facebook feed not so long ago. Sometimes the Universe works in mysterious ways.

The path to healing and regaining your self-esteem and self-love is a lengthy and tough journey, often marked by many detours. You may sometimes question, as I did, whether this is advisable. You are still dented and crumpled, just like the old $100 note, but you are worth the difficulty it takes to find yourself again. I found it useful to plot how I'd reach my destination. As a teacher, I worked on setting goals and writing the strategies and resources I'd used to achieve these. Once I was receiving therapy and was able to cognitively function better, I put this plan in place, and it helped. I felt a sense of achievement when I was able to tick off things, whether they were as extensive as goals or as minor as items on my daily to-do list.

I celebrated my small achievements rather than struggling to see the big picture. That was too difficult at that time. Getting out of bed and having a shower, even though I often felt drained at the end and needed to rest, earned me a star. Changing my bedding each week earned me two stars. You can see my teacher's brain at work here. I started walking my dog to the park once a day at first and definitely needed a nana nap after that. I was rewarded two stars for that mammoth effort. When I made that twice a day, even if I drove to the park, I decided it was worth another star. My reward came with twenty stars.

The reward I chose was an outing to a café for coffee and carrot cake, my favourite. The secret to rewards is that they must be what you want. I not only wanted but needed a good cup of coffee rather than the instant stuff. The cake, a no-brainer. All I needed to do was accept it. This was more difficult for me as I had rarely left the unit for months. However, the calling of brewed coffee and the cake I love most in the world, along with finding a café I doubted Arse would visit, made it worth it. It meant I was able to escape from what felt like a prison and relax to some degree for a short time. Then the anxiety and need to be in familiar territory claimed me.

Each time I did this exercise, I tried to stay out of the village confines longer. After a month or so, I even took a book to read. Yes, I had started reading again, mainly self-help books suggested to me. I also started to go to cafés near the sea, which has always been my happy place. All this was noted down in a diary so I could plot my recovery, similar to a teacher's marks book, which I showed when I presented for my therapy sessions.

The most important thing to remember here is not to give yourself grief if you have a fall. Pick yourself up, dust yourself off, reset and start again.

Empowering affirmations are beneficial on this journey. They are like your cheering squad. Their role is to reframe negative thoughts and replace them with a positive self-image. Sometimes this is more difficult than reading and saying the words seem. Affirmations need to be practised regularly, generally at least once a day. If I were having a difficult time dealing with something, usually after being tormented by Arse, I grabbed my cards, put on my headphones and played some soothing music while I read and spoke the affirmations I thought most apt.

These wonderful, short phrases strengthen self-esteem, help reduce stress and alleviate feelings of inadequacy. They're also beneficial in building resilience and supporting a mindset of growth. This contributes to our well-being and emotional strength. I still incorporate them into my daily routine, often upon rising and along with giving thanks for the freedom I have now.

In her book, *Women Who Love Too Much* (Reprinted by Penguin Books 2022), Robin Norwood shares her belief that beginning the day with this simple affirmation, *(Your Name), I love you and accept you exactly the way you are,* addresses both the most important and most difficult issues many women have. This has shades of what Mark Darcy (Colin Firth) said to Bridget Jones (Renee Zellweger) in the original Bridget Jones movie: '*I like you just the way you are.*' I have adopted my version of that, 'I like me just the way I am', which I say when negative thoughts try to permeate my brain.

Some of my other favourites are:

- I am at peace with my past.
- I am letting go of that which no longer brings me happiness.
- I am confident I will achieve my goals.
- I am embracing self-love and self-worth.
- I am a resilient and strong woman.

I have printed out these and pasted them into my journal, with another copy on the inside of my wardrobe door to be seen every morning. This is what I needed to do. However, I understand it's not everyone's cup of tea. It's about whatever you feel comfortable with and which helps in your recovery, your journey and you finding and loving yourself again.

Whenever I come across another gem, I write it in my journal. I have also purchased several card packs of affirmations for different situations. These are great to BluTak onto the bathroom mirror, behind the toilet door or keep, as I do, in the top drawer of my bedside table. Before I go to sleep, I randomly select a card and read it. As I drift off to sleep, I have it going through my mind on repeat, hoping to wake calm and refreshed.

However, my favourite of all is the 'Serenity Prayer'. It is one of the most famous prayers, written by Reinhold Niebuhr in the 1800s. In the 1940s, it was adopted in a shortened version by Alcoholics Anonymous as part of their recovery program. This prayer was my salvation in the early weeks after the rape when I was not in a very good space at all.

Serenity Prayer

'God, grant me the serenity to accept the things I cannot change.
The courage to change the things I can.
And, the wisdom to know the difference.'

It was the only thing I knew to do at that time, not having the benefit of therapy for at least four months after the rape.

Accepting change is difficult at the best of times, for some more than others. I was one of those people who lived by the notion that *'if it isn't broken, don't fix it'*, an expression common in the 1970s, the era of my high school and university years. You can, however, learn to accept change in your life.

The first thing is to let go.

Basically, it is forgiving yourself and moving on. In 'How to Let Go of the Things of the Past', (Sara Lindburg, 21 March 2023, www.healthline.com), she outlined:

Twelve Tips for Letting Go

1. Have a positive mantra to say, especially when you need to reframe your thoughts
2. Creating a physical, and therefore a psychological distance, will help in not being reminded about the person or situation
3. Focus on yourself and something you are grateful for, so you remain positive
4. The more you focus on the present, the less the past controls you
5. Be gentle with yourself, as kindness and compassion are what is needed.

6. Let feelings of negative emotions flow out, rather than keeping them bottled in
7. You may never receive an apology, so don't wait for it by moving on with your life
8. Self-care, such as saying no and putting your needs first, as well as immersing yourself in what brings you happiness, is a priority
9. Surround yourself with people who care and support you
10. Talking it out is very important; therefore, give yourself permission to do so
11. Giving yourself permission to forgive allows you to let go of anger, guilt, shame, etc.
12. Experienced professionals, therapists, psychologists, etc., will guide you through this process

Some of these I have achieved, while others are definitely a work in progress! Finding your true self again, particularly after a traumatic event, is often a long, but definitely arduous, task. It is well worth it, and I, for one, will keep working on myself... probably for the rest of my days.

About a year ago, I read *The Let Them Theory* by Mel Robbins, and it seriously changed my life. It is a huge worldwide phenomenon. However, few know 'Let Them' was actually a poem written by Cassie Phillips, along with many of her writings, that formed the basis of The Let Them Movement, which started in 2020. Part of this poem is at the end of the chapter. She summed up the movement through these words:

> '*Remember—We cannot control the actions of others, but we can choose how we respond. Choose kindness and forgiveness, but not at the risk of losing yourself to another's storm. Love and respect yourself enough to decide when to brave the storm or seek shelter. It's okay to Let go and Let Them, so you can finally and unapologetically Let You.*' www.cassie-phillips.com

The premise of the book is that if you ever feel frustrated, overwhelmed or stuck in one place, the problem isn't with you. It is the power you give to others to hold over you. Therefore, by using two simple words, *Let Them*, you cut the ties, opinions, drama and judgment to free yourself from this negative cycle. There is also a Facebook group, and people often add their poems to this page. I have used many as a source of encouragement when needed.

Why does this resonate with me? As a constant reminder to myself, I have 'Let Go' tattooed on the inside wrist of my left arm and 'Let Them' tattooed in the same place on my right arm. I see them several times a day, and they remind me to stop, breathe and give thanks for how far I have come from those early dark days of December 2021. It has been a tough journey, one I hope no one else needs to travel down. Frighteningly, statistics tell me differently.

I have confidence this, too, will resonate with you. Letting go of things you can't control goes a long way to freeing yourself from the stress, anxiety and unnecessary conflict that has become part of your life. You need to believe, as I have, that this is a possibility. Believe that true empowerment only comes through knowing when to let go and when to take action. Only you can decide which path you will take in any situation. Giving yourself permission to do so is a huge step forward.

I hope you can find consolation, help and peace as you read my book. And there are many others like it. The more books I read, the more resilient I became until I was able to break the chains that held me for so long. It will be an ongoing battle. I still have my not-so-great days, but now I know that's normal. I give myself permission to grieve for a while before bringing myself back to the present, where I need to be.

It's about releasing the control others have over you and focusing on the things you can change, as is so beautifully stated in the 'Serenity Prayer'. So, adopt this, if it speaks to you, and other affirmations you connect with. Let them take away the noises and voices in your head when you are overwhelmed again and are spiralling down. Let them be the strength you need to face your fears and move forward. Let them be the light to guide you to a better place, a safer place. Let them.

Just Let Them

If they want to choose something or someone over you, LET THEM.
If they want to go weeks without talking to you, LET THEM.
If they are okay with never seeing you, LET THEM.
If they are okay with always putting themselves first, LET THEM.
If they are showing you who they are and not what you perceived them to be, LET THEM.
If they want to follow the crowd, LET THEM.
If they want to judge or misunderstand you, LET THEM.
If they act like they can live without YOU, LET THEM.
If they want to walk out of your life and leave, LET THEM.
Hold open the door, AND LET THEM.

Let them lose you.
You were never theirs, because you were always your own.
So LET THEM.

Cassie Phillips

Chapter 11

Wash Away the Dirt and Love Me, Warts and All

———————— ◆◇◆ ————————

Survivors of any and all abuse become very good at anticipating the mood of others, looks, actions, all of it in an effort to survive. Believing that if we can become compliant and loving, do things how they want, that we will become safe. This becomes our way of life.
Darlene Ouimet, www.healthyplace.com

Instead of being compliant, imagine making the decision to leave a toxic relationship and start a ripple effect of change. It would be like dominoes, lined up in a pattern and ready to fall once the first one is tapped.

All choices have the potential to reshape your life. This will shift the negative energy as you move forward to bring about the necessary positive change. As I have said before, it won't be easy. It will take everything you can give, and then some. And to be honest, there may be times when you're ready to throw in the towel and go back to the place that is familiar, even if it is not safe. Joyce Rachelle summed this up in a post on www.happierhuman.com:

> *'Some scars don't hurt. Some scars are numb. Some scars rid you of the capacity to feel anything ever again.'*

When you leave the intimate personal bond that has harmed your being, it will be difficult to accept that you will now be alone and no longer in a partnership, that, even if it wasn't mutually beneficial, was somehow often better than nothing. Being with a narcissist will have conditioned your way of thinking and damaged your individuality. Therefore, you will need to change how you view the path you can take as a single person. It will possibly one of the most difficult choices you ever make.

However, it will be the one thing that makes you stronger and more resilient. I can only encourage you to take the first step to a better life, free from the abuse you had been forced to accept.

Lyndon B Johnson, 36th President of the United States of America, 1963-1969, said,

> *'Yesterday is not ours to recover, but tomorrow is ours to win or lose.'*

This simple but apt quote reminds us to look forward when we leave the controlling narcissist, because looking back may make it harder to walk away. This is what they are counting on. My suggestion is to pre-play in your mind what you are going to do, if you are mentally strong enough to do so, in order to make this scenario possible. Having an endplay is what helped me take the first steps towards my freedom.

To help you, it may be wise to listen to family and/or friends and seek their advice. Many haven't said anything to you about your partner, even when they think he is a fucking dickhead. They do this as they want to be supportive and don't want to offend you. Or they shut up because you were always defending him. This certainly is what happened in my case. All those times Arse invited himself when I was meeting with my colleagues or comrades, they held their counsel. My family stayed quiet, believing it was what I would have wanted. As one of my sons said, in a loving way, I had a shocking track record in choosing men. However, this time, they must speak their truth when you ask. If everyone had shown less politeness, it could have saved me a lot of mental and emotional anguish and more possible physical abuse if I had stayed longer than I did.

The time you start to walk your path alone will feel strange. It will be exceptionally tough; however, these times are the ones to build your character and make you stronger after your traumatic experiences. Once you take the first steps, keep going. Use all your senses to help ground you again.

Hold your head up and look around you, taking in the scenery that has been so long denied. See the colours and the angles that make patterns in your surroundings. Smell the fresh air and draw it deeply into your lungs. Let it purify all that was tainted before and exhale it. Listen to the sounds that may be strange to your ears, but try to pick out your song in them. The one with the lyrics that say, *I'm free*. Touch the things that were once familiar, but during your captivity, you lost the sensation of them. Let your fingers linger over the textures to reignite in your mind the connections they inspired. Lastly, taste your freedom. You may ask how this is possible, but you can. Remember all those luxurious flavours that delighted your taste buds.

WASH AWAY THE DIRT AND LOVE ME, WARTS AND ALL

You can have them again, and they will be even better, sharper and more wonderful than previously. All this is inside you, waiting for you to spread your wings again and fly away to your new life.

Now you understand you have the know-how, and you believe you can do it; half the battle is won. There are no more excuses you can make. Yes, you may well be terrified. Yes, you may wonder what the ramifications will be. Yes, you will be alone to start again, though hopefully with the support of others. Yes, life as you know it will be different... of that there is no doubt.

> *'Overcoming abuse doesn't just happen. It takes positive steps every day. Let today be the day you start to move forward'* (Assunta Harris, www.healthplaces.com).

You walk away and stay away because you finally value your own worth. Mine was a difficult journey, as most are, but once I'd started, the momentum kept me going. It's like training for a marathon. You don't start running 42 kilometres every day as training. You'd never finish the first time you tried to do that. You need to have a strategy which incorporates a fitness routine, often gym work, before building up the distance you would run over a long period of time. So, once I'd decided to move forward, I knew I needed to see it through to completion… regaining my freedom, and along with it my strength and will to never allow this to happen again.

In Chapter 8, I listed thirteen ways to get over a narcissist, as outlined on www.choosingtherapy.com. Number eleven is *'being mindful of moving on too quickly.'* Sage advice, and I wish I had taken it to heart. It seems, however, that I was still very vulnerable. Through a third source, I met a man whose path I had crossed but hadn't been aware of at that time. He had a university degree, and we were both in the same profession. I thought, for once, I'd won the jackpot. We had so much in common, and he made me laugh. This was something that hadn't happened in a long time. It was fast and fiery, and I was caught up… again, in the overwhelming sensation of being attracted to someone, even when I had vowed to remain single forever. Having someone give you compliments, who wanted to talk with you at least twice a day, and for long sessions at a time, while inundating you with texts throughout your day, was a great ego boost and not something I'd really ever experienced.

I hadn't even heard of love bombing before I did my research on narcissistic behaviours. It is like a match when it's first lit. It sparks brightly. As the match burns down to the end of the wood, it starts to fizzle out. This is what love bombing is like; it is not real love, which is complicated and requires time to thrive.

> *'Initially, you might feel safe, secure and swept off your feet because grand gestures are a self-esteem boost and make you feel important and desired. But the love bomber's ultimate goal is not just to seek love, but to gain control over someone else. Over time, those grand gestures are an effort to manipulate you and make you feel indebted to and dependent on them.'* www.health-clevelandclinic.org, psychologist Alaina Tiani, PhD., "What is Love Bombing?" February 1, 2023.

However, the compliments go to your head, the attention is magic and you feel like a woman again, and an attractive one at that. Well, I did, and it was wonderful. I had a reason to smile, with that sexy twinkle in my eye. But I was falling into the same patterns, I just didn't realise it. I didn't understand that I was being pressured to surrender so quickly and that our relationship would almost be exclusive, cutting out time with family and friends, as had been my signature response previously. I had just replaced one type of emotional abuse and control with another. And all within eighteen months of breaking free of Arse and settling away from Perth.

I thought Mr Nice Guy could be the one, even though there were a few alarm bells and red flags. I ignored those. I'd had therapy and thought I knew what I was letting myself in for. For an academic, I'm a pretty easy target. This is not something to be proud of. Even before he called it time on our relationship, around the year-and-a-half mark, he was on an online dating site, looking for an Asian 'bride' to replace me, and he had been in contact with her as well. We had definitely stepped through the three stages of the love bombing relationship:

1. **The Idealisation Phase:** You are swept off your feet by the compliments, attention, gifts and loving actions. I was like a flower, opening up to the sunshine.
2. **The Devaluation Phase:** Once you are comfortable, they begin their campaign to control you, often in a subtle way, sometimes in an abusive way. This is where his sexual fetishes became apparent, and he was like a spoiled schoolboy if I was non-compliant.
3. **The Discard Phase:** Just as it says, you don't comply, then it's bye-bye. And it was, leaving me feeling, once again, like a failure.

'When it ends, you might have conflicting emotions because while you've had this attachment or love for the person who love bombed you, you also might feel anger or sadness about how things went down.

> *Often, they will try to come back and repeat the process by checking in with you—and that's when you run the risk of getting sucked back in.'*
> www.health-clevelandclinic.org, Dr Tiani, 'What is Love Bombing?' February 1, 2023

If it wasn't for that relationship, I doubt I would have seen why it is so important to take heed of the warning not to form a relationship before you are fully over the trauma and embarrassment and you can live independently and alone as a functioning adult. There is no timeline for this. I have met some women during my study for writing this book who have grieved the end of their relationship while still in it, so that they walked free and were ready to take on the world as soon as they closed the door behind them. Others are still fixated on the wrongs done to them many years after being out of the relationship. Personally, I don't think this is healthy as they have obviously not reconciled everything in their mind and could do with some more counselling to help them over their hump. I believe I'm somewhere in between, still sitting on the fence!

What did I do? I went back and spoke with people about it, both professionals and friends. This time, I really listened to a few painful home truths. I think that was almost more difficult than knowing I had been replaced before our connection was severed. It did, however, open my eyes and made me realise that I had to work on myself. It was a bitter pill to swallow, but because I had come so far since the rape, and I'm as tenacious as a dog after a bone; I refused to believe I was a failure. I used this experience as a stepping stone to get back on track. It feels good... really good. Now, to continue as I have started.

How did I do that? I went back and researched as much as I could on narcissism and its behaviours. I watched and listened to numerous podcasts, and I talked with people I'd met in some of my therapy groups. You need both the theoretical side as well as the stories others had lived during the abuse they received to get a well-rounded picture.

Where to from here? Isn't that the six-million-dollar question? I have a few ideas in mind.

First, I want to get my story out to you and as many people as I can so that you all know you are not alone if you have been or still are in any type of abusive, narcissistic relationship.

Secondly, I hope some of the information I have included, such as where to go for help and how to understand what narcissism is and the way it can impact people's lives, is valuable to you. As are the strategies for moving forward with your life once the decision has been made to break free from the unhealthy and abusive relationship in which you have surrendered yourself, willingly or otherwise.

Thirdly, with the knowledge I have amassed and my degree as a teacher, I'd love to go on a speaking circuit and run workshops for those wanting to, or who have already, escaped the tyranny of narcissism.

Fourthly, I want to give a voice for you and those who have been silenced, so you understand there are people, like myself, who are willing to reach out and speak for you when you can't.

Lastly, I will be writing a second book about my journey from self-loathing to self-loving, and how the damage to my inner child was the root cause of why I was often attracted to those with narcissistic traits or who are under the banner of narcissistic personality disorder (NPD).

In conclusion, I reiterate… Be kind to yourself. Be gentle with yourself. Be focused on staying on your path for freedom: freedom from ongoing trauma, freedom from abuse and, most importantly, freedom from the pressure and guilt you put on yourself. Only you can do this.

> *A note to anyone who needs to hear it: We don't "get over" or "move on" from our trauma. We are forced to make space for it. We carry it. We learn to live with it. And, sometimes we thrive in spite of it. Unknown, Youth Dynamics, www.yd.org*

Chapter 12

It's a Wrap

---◆◇◆---

> *The role of a writer is not to say what we all can say, but what we are unable to say.*
> *Anäis Nin, www.quotesgram.com*

This is a short story I wrote for a competition in my local area. As I have said previously, writing is a great way to say what you want to share, whether you share it with others or not. This time I DEFINITELY wanted others to know my story. And what a great way to get it out there.

The Year of the Snake

The year 1953 was the Year of the Snake in Chinese astrology. It was also the birth year of a person of dubious character who was a part of my life for over five, oh-so very long years. A Snake is a snake, and my Snake was as typical as one gets. Only this Piggy, with my squinty little eyes, saw past his hidden bad traits and looked for his best side, his soft underbelly. I hate snakes, hate them with a passion, always have and always will. I've been known to change channels when they appear on television, and there is no way in hell I would ever go near one or hold one of the slimy, slithery creatures.

It's no wonder they have such a bad reputation. We've all watched *Raiders of the Lost Ark* and *Snakes on a Plane,* which I only paid attention to in order to drool over Harrison Ford and Samuel L Jackson. I'm sure there are other movies featuring snakes I haven't been forced to see... thank goodness. I'm not sure my heart could take much more, no matter how gorgeous the leading man was.

In my defence, I didn't know the new man who was entering my life was a Snake. My bad!

It has been said that the Snake is renowned for being cautious and often an introverted observer, who can be deemed mysterious due to their usually suspicious and insecure nature. Moreover, they are typically emotionally

IT'S A WRAP

detached, which manifests as coldness, selfishness and insensitivity. Ain't that the truth! Many people distrust them because they appear calculating and are entirely focused on their own welfare. In romance, the Snake struggles to be vulnerable, protecting themselves with their usual detachment, which often spells failure. However, because he thinks of himself as Prince Charming, he may face many temptations throughout his life, such as having someone on the sidelines to replace the victim with whom he is tired of playing.

That man, my Snake, ticked all those boxes... and many more.

He was a snake. He was one of the most venomous snakes a person could be. He could be likened to a king cobra that hunts other snakes, even its own species. He certainly sought out females with a tenacity born of need. Or he could be seen as a taipan, which moves quickly and strikes fiercely, several times. He was one to never let an opportunity pass him by. Personally, I believe he was the eastern brown snake reincarnated. When threatened, he would rise up—he was all of five feet six inches in the old height measurement—and open his mouth in a vicious display. What followed would have made his mother turn in her grave.

On the flip side, I was born in the Year of the Pig. Our motto is *good things come to those who wait,* and I was so silly and infatuated that I believed everything was rosy when I first met him. To say he wasn't the sharpest knife in my cutlery drawer wasn't far from the truth; however, he was different to the other men with whom I'd had an *expired* relationship. I prefer this term to failed relationship as it means I've served my time and was free to leave. That is not the most appropriate way to view a relationship, apparently, but it works for me and seemed positive after years of singledom.

He was fit and nicely built for someone his age, though he was a bit of a peacock who loved to flaunt his gym-sculpted physique. The bonus was he didn't seem to mind, at *that* time, that I had a fuller figure, shall we say. It sounds better than two stone overweight, especially as we Piggies like to eat, often gorging ourselves, even if it does come back to bite us later!

To our credit though, Piggies are generally seen as very social and highly communicative, a foil for his more hesitant and reticent nature. I had many friends, he had few. Those whom he called friends seemed to dominate him, particularly one work colleague. Interestingly enough, I later learned that he, too, was a Snake. While my Snake was more covert, one who would only strike if in danger, his mate was definitely overt, domineering and always on the lookout for some action. It wasn't long before the mate was guiding him along a path to where the big Snakes would play. Trouble was rearing its ugly head, like

IT'S A WRAP

a Cobra ready to strike. And, when it appeared, I was in the firing line.

I'm a true Piggie, not just because of the eating! I'm pragmatic and realistic, most of the time, and work with great ambition and perseverance towards my true aspirations. I'd give 100% of myself to any task, and I expected my partner to be the same. At first, he seemed to do that. Then I started to realise he was extremely good at appearing to be focused and on task, when, in all honesty, he was just a great actor. Honestly, he could have won an Oscar and a BAFTA, as well as several Logies, for his performances.

He looked as if he was working, but he was one of those people who would walk around an office carrying a file and pen, stopping to speak with others, writing things down, using the photocopier and generally faffing around. Except he didn't work in an office. He drove a truck, so he checked the pressure of the numerous tyres at least twice, pulled on the straps to ensure they were taut, and went through the paperwork, as keenly as an examiner scrutinises an exam paper, before he even started the engine for the necessary ten-minute warm-up.

As he was paid an hourly rate, and I'm pretty sure he charged for overtime every single week of his working life. And he religiously took smoko breaks, and a few sneaky sleeps under a tree where he couldn't be seen. It seems

I wasn't the only one fooled. Though when you appear simple and don't rock the company boat, you can easily fly under the radar. Or should that be slither under the truck? Whatever... he did it well.

Piggies are not known to be cowardly or weak. They certainly wouldn't be the captain who abandoned the ship before the passengers, nor would they back off from danger. Additionally, they are sensitive to the plight of others and abhor the unjust mistreatment of those who are intentionally ostracised and isolated. All challenges would be met with boldness and impunity, ready to face off against those who got in their way. I believed I demonstrated those qualities: a person who fought for the underdog and was determined and responsible in this regard. This may sound like something I'd write in my curriculum vitae; in fact, I think that's where I pinched it from.

I thought my Snake was a person of this calibre as well. How sadly mistaken and deluded I was. I know I wear rose-coloured lenses in my glasses, but I didn't realise they hid his worst traits from me. I am sure many of his ideas and beliefs were word-perfect from the Snake Leader, as I nicknamed his mate, which he tried to pass off as his own. My Snake wasn't that intelligent, though he was good at remembering things and repeating them, even if the meaning flew over his head like a flock of birds. Snake Leader was very cagey and very smart. He would say something for my Snake to impart to me.

IT'S A WRAP

These snippets of information were innocuous at first, and I let them *go through to the keeper,* as the saying goes, rather than make a deal about it. After all, I am also a Libra—the peacekeeper. Gradually, however, what was said and how it was told to me changed. My Snake changed. He had shed his skin, and the new layer was thicker, like an armour. He was coiled, ready to strike at any time. Everything seemed to aggravate him... especially me. I started to see his true colours. He wasn't one of those snakes with beautiful colours and markings. No, he was brown, the colour of shit. That's what he was... a shit-coloured snake disguised as a shitty man.

And this was when I realised the Snake and the Pig were not compatible romantic partners and probably wouldn't be friends either. So, I did what any self-respecting person who believes in the zodiac and Chinese zodiac signs does: I Googled Libra and Leo, Snake and Pig. And didn't Wikipedia come up with some fascinating information for me! I obviously should have done my homework earlier—a red cross for this teacher, and quite possibly a detention as well. As I'm old enough for the time when five thrashings of the cane across the palm of your hand were allowed, I'd probably be up for those too.

The Snake and the Pig are the worst match. Apparently, and hindsight is a marvellous thing, quarrelling would be the least of the couple's problems. There was also a potential for violence, so someone, obviously the Libra Pig rather than the Leo Snake, was going to get hurt until they split.

Once I, the Libra Pig, needed to rebalance my scales, the ones that are used for weighing rather than the armour on the snake, I found my voice and used it. That was not appreciated at all. *NO, no, no... that is not allowed*, hissed the Snake Leader. *The man is in charge of the house, and the little woman must be dutiful in every way.* I know we were born in the 1950s; I didn't think we still had to abide by the ways things were done in that era.

It was the little things at first that I started to notice. He wanted to be with me all the time. If I wanted to go shopping, he thought he'd come too. Fair enough if he wanted to do his own thing and then meet up for coffee and lunch later. But no, he walked with me into every shop, like a dog following its owner... just not as well-behaved. If I picked up an item of clothing, he'd look over my shoulder at the tag. First, to check the sizing, and secondly, to check the price, even if I were to pay with it from my personal account. I had learned way back not to try things on in the shop, as he always wanted to be in the changeroom with me. Most are barely big enough for one, let alone him being there to criticise the colour or pattern, and most definitely the fit. He was over being polite, and body shaming became the norm, never backwards in coming forward about my body and its post-baby flab.

IT'S A WRAP

My youngest may be in her thirties, but one can't rush into getting fit again after giving birth! That was the only thing he was bright enough to figure out by himself, so he 'lovingly' paid for me, as my birthday present no less, to work with his personal trainer three times a week. *Be still, my beating heart*! That's how to endear yourself to a woman! If I hadn't realised the honeymoon phase was over, that was what toppled the figurines of the bride and groom from the top tier of the cake! Then I started keeping score.

Snake 1, Pig 0.

Wait, there's more... just like the Demtel advert. He started comparing me to his late wife, the one he married, literally, on her deathbed. When he told me he proposed to her after thirty-three years together, I thought that was so romantic and sweet. Then, a few years later, I realised she hadn't left a will, and her name was on the title deed of the house. The only way to stop her children and grandchildren from claiming her estate was to marry her. That way, 100% goes to the spouse. How's that for a snakey move? He was either smarter than I gave him credit for, or someone informed him of this. I believe it was the latter. And the Snake struck again! Another point to him.

Snake 2, Pig 0.

Then it was, 'My wife always wore makeup. You'd look prettier if you did too.' Another beauty I recall is, 'My wife kept the house immaculate...' Yep, and I was still working four days a week while he was retired. The Snake didn't have a clue how to use the dishwasher, the vacuum cleaner or the washing machine, and had no interest in learning, so was unable to assist with such menial tasks. Silly me, there was plenty of time between midnight and six in the morning when I could have done all those chores instead of sleeping. What was I thinking?

Obviously, I wasn't... as most of my friends asked after the Snake V Pig showdown with lawyers. They were on to him from the get-go. It's a pity no one warned me before his accountant and the Snake himself strongly suggested I transfer my superannuation into his self-managed fund. I was given the fancy title of co-director. Woopy-doo! It meant little in the long run. He got the house, the car and the new furniture. This was after it was mostly my furniture that had been sold when we downsized, although the money did go towards the new furniture... which he kept.

And let's not forget to mention that it was my car that was sold, as he believed we only needed one after I retired. He had this little Piggy totally hog-tied and roasting nicely on a spit over very hot coal. And he continued to baste me until I was done to his satisfaction. I was losing the game badly and couldn't see a way to score a point. As he received two points.

IT'S A WRAP

The scoreboard read, Snake 4, Pig 0.

Shall I discuss the thinly veiled threats that had started? Or the fact that he would drive me to where I was going to meet friends before coming in to say hello. He wasn't being polite. He was a Snake and didn't trust that I wasn't seeing another man. As if... one was bad enough! More often than not, he invited himself to lunch as well. *How embarrassment*! as Effie Stephanidis from *Acropolis Now* would say. I'd just smile weakly and wished the earth would open up and swallow me. Instead, this time my Snake had transformed into an anaconda and had me for lunch.

On the scoreboard, it was Snake 5, Pig 0.

On another occasion, when I was going to meet my sister in Hobart for a week's rest and relaxation, he was extremely angry that we both said he couldn't come. He even rang my brother-in-law to see what he thought about the situation and was told by him to calm down. He was NOT a very happy snake and recoiled, ready to strike at me. It was a bitter attack. I felt his venomous words pierce me like his fangs would have.

When that failed to stop me from going, or make my sister and I let him join our holiday, he met with one of my sons, without my knowledge at that time. He, too, told him to chill out, that smothering me like a python squeezing its prey was not a way to deal with his strong, independent mother. To say that didn't go as planned is an understatement. Although I was ferociously bitten again, I had made a score on the board, which now reads, Snake 5, Pig 1.

And I had a great time with my sister, ate lots, shopped up a storm on our joint account, and this not-so-little Piggy went *wee, wee, wee,* metaphorically speaking, all the way home.

I was catching up. Snake 5, Pig 2. I had this... I was on a roll.

Or not! I arrived home to find the large photo of him and his late wife hanging pride of place as you walked in the front door. This was after I was told I had to Uber it home as he was busy. He was busy, going out to the theatre with another woman, no less. What's more amazing is that he was able to book the tickets online himself, something he had never been able to do previously. Well played, Snake, well played. I know we'd been sleeping in separate bedrooms for about six months, since he physically attacked me, but I didn't expect he could slither any closer to the ground.

He was awarded two points for his entrepreneurial skills, bringing the totals to Snake 7, Pig 2.

IT'S A WRAP

A Piggy knows when she is cooked, with the crackling just right, and I was done perfectly. All that was required was lashings of apple sauce and mountains of roast vegetables, and I was a dish being served to him on a platter. This Piggy may have had a tough hide, but it was no match for the fangs of this venomous Snake.

The moral of this story is beware of the Snake. Some may be fine if they're small pythons, and you keep them as pets... if you're so inclined. Personally, I'd be wary of all Snakes, as you never know when they could strike. Stay clear of the bigger ones, the venomous ones, or those that squeeze the shit out of you. Be on your guard, watch where you go, and for Heaven's sake, ask a man you fancy what his Chinese zodiac sign is. If he is a Snake, run away as quickly as you can before he bites or snares you.

Especially if you are a Piggy.

Annie Chandler, July 2025, Big Sky Writing Festival

Conclusion

---◆◇◆---

> *Their adventures happen in the springtime when one moment snow is falling and the sun shines the next, which is also a little like life—it can turn on a sixpence. I hope this book encourages you, perhaps, to live courageously with more kindness for yourself and others. And to ask for help when you need it—which is always a brave thing to do... the truth is everyone is winging it.*
> *The Boy, the Mole, the Fox and the Horse,*
> *Charlie Mackesy*

IT IS NOT YOUR FAULT. You were conditioned, often without your awareness, until things constricted around you, like tight-fitting clothing squeezing you until it is difficult to breathe. Be aware of the red flags and DO NOT ignore them. This is so easy to do, I know. However, now you are conscious of them, use your senses. If anything seems, sounds, or feels off, listen to your intuition... it is your protective armour you have hopefully built up. Remember what a narcissist is and how they play their game. *A word to the wise is enough. The old proverb is, forewarned, forearmed* (Captain Francis Hooke, The History of New Hampshire, 1685).

Now you know how toxic relationships can easily become, live life on your terms. Love yourself, warts and all, as well as being kind to yourself. Most of us take on the guilt of the narcissist, when it is not ours to carry. It's their baggage and, if they don't want it, let them leave it on the unclaimed luggage rack.

Keep your boundaries. You have built those walls to protect; they are there for this purpose, so DO NOT let anyone break them down. Know what you will and will not accept, and understand your reasoning for each. Be STRONG. This is the most important way to stay safe.

If you are not at the stage where you totally believe you are capable of making the right decision, knowing some of the unhealthy ones you made in the past, call on the support team you have gathered to help you... and listen to them, and actively hear what they have to say. There is no shame is requiring help, especially when you have been burnt before.

CONCLUSION

Be EMPOWERED:

- Go to therapy.
- Use your affirmations.
- Seek assistance.
- Any knowledge, particularly about narcissism, is powerful—read and research.
- Do things you enjoy, that give you positives in your life, as you deserve them.
- Distance yourself from the situation wherever possible—it is easier to build a new life in a different place.
- Use the help lines listed in Chapter 5.
- Pray, to whatever God or Higher Being you believe in.

To end this book, I will share this poem I came across, by accident, when I was looking for something completely different. The Universe was shining its light on me. I hope you let the message resonate with you, too.

YOU ARE NOT ALONE

I Owe an Apology to the Younger Me

*I wish I could go back and
wrap my arms around you,
Whisper that it will all be okay,
And remind you of your worth.
I wish I could hand you the strength you needed
to speak up,
To walk away and to never settle for less than
you deserved.*

*But then I remember... every scar, every
heartbreak, every battle
Shaped me into the woman I am today.
And for that, I carry both grief and gratitude.*

www.facebook.com, Thee Misfit Momma

Be kind and gentle with yourself. Life happens. Learn from it and move forward, even if it is slowly, inch by inch. Smile in the face of adversity. Stand proud. You are worthy.

Much love,

Annie

Thank You

References

Australian Bureau of Statistics: www.abs.gov.au/statistics/detailed-methodology-information/concepts-sources-methods/personal-safety-survey-user-guide/2021-22/par

Better Help Therapy: https://betterhelp.com

Hill, Jess: *See What You Made Me Do,* Black Inc Books, Australia, June 2019

Lindburg, Sara: *How to Let Go of the Things of the Past*, Healthline.com, https://healthline.com

Mackesy, Charlie: *The Boy, the Mole, the Fox and the Horse,* Penguin Random House, UK 2019

Article by Louise Morales-Brown: *Coercive Control,* Medical News Today, June 29, 2020 https://www.medicalnewstoday.com

Norwood, Robin: *Women Who Love Too Much,* Penguin Random House, UK 2022 (update and reprint)

Robbins, Mel: *The Let Them Theory: A Life-Changing Tool that Millions of People Can't Stop Talking About,* Amplify Publishing, USA December, 2024

Online Sites:

A-Z Quotes: Shakti Gawain (author and teacher), https://www.azquotes.com

Carla Corelli: *Healing After Narcissistic Abuse,* https://carlacorelli.com

Cleveland Clinic: Grace Tworek PsyD, *Understanding Narcissism,* https://myclevelandclinic.org/podcasts/health-essentials/understanding-narcissism-with-grace-tworek

Choosing Therapy: https://www.choosingtherapy.com/?s=how+to+get+over+a+narcissist

Healthy Place: https://www.healthyplace.com

Dr Elayna Fernandez, *The Positive Mom*: https://thepositivemom.com/the-narcissists-prayer

REFERENCES

Mindset Made Better: https://mindsetmadebetter.com

Beattie Melody: *Minding Therapy*, https://mindingtherapy.com

Phillips, Cassie: Poem: *Let Them,* https://www.cassie-phillips.com

Psychology Made Better: https://psychologytoday.com

Quote Fancy: https://quotefancy.com

Quotes I Love: https://www.quotesilove/it-takes-time-to-heal-a-broken-heart-quotes

Quotes Gram: https://quotesgram.com

The Daily OM, 1996 onwards, articles and courses http://www.dailyOM.com

The Daily Wellness, 2025 http://thedailywellness.com

The Narcissist Hunters, https://thenarcissisthunters.com/blog/

Thinking Therapy, *Keys to Stopping* by Melody Beattie www.thinkingtherapy.com

Youth Dynamics, https://www.yd.org

Udemy courses: *Triumph After Narcissistic Abuse* by Beth Anne Ferris-Palinginis, *The Narcissistic Survival Kit: Tools for Empowerment* by Dani Bonilla www.udemy.com

Bennett-Henry, Stephanie: 50 Quotes, It's Okay Not To Be Okay, https://quotement.com/its-okay-not-to-be-okay-quotes

Facebook Sources:

Consiglio, Maria: *Understanding the Narc,* https://www.facebook.com/understandingthenarc

Fifty Shades of Tired, https://www.facebook.com/FiftyShadesOfTired#

If You Miss Me: March 26 2025 https://www.facebook.com/N.Miss.Me/posts/1218056216350334

Mathew Martorana: https://www.facebook.com/mathewmartorana

Narcissist Abuse Survivors, www.facebook.com/narcissistabusesurvivors

North, Ryan: *The Minds Journal* www.facebook.com/themindsjournal

REFERENCES

Silent Writings: *Leave Before You Forget Who You Are*, May 28, 2025 https://www.facebook.com/silentwritings

Thee Misfit Momma: I Owe an Apology to the Younger Me, https://www.facebook.com/TheeMisfitMomma

Sources:

Car, Edward: *Values for Success,* Pennon Publishing, Australia, 2003

Van Cuylenburg, Hugh: *The Resilience Project: Finding Happiness Through Gratitude, Empathy & Mindfulness,* Penguin Random House, Australia, 2019

Acknowledgements

First and foremost, my thanks go to Natasa and Stuart Denham and all the wonderful crew of Ultimate 48 Hour Author for your guidance, support and knowledge in assisting me to get this book from a seed of an idea when I attended your masterclass in Perth, March 2025 to this published book nine months later. I could not have done it without your fantastic outline, the three-day retreat and the weekly Zoom accountability sessions. Not to mention having the assistance of Julie and Vivi only an email or a phone call away. I've already signed up for the Ultimate Package, so I will be writing many more books in the future.

To Nikola Boskovski who has set up my landing page and website. That was no mean feat when dealing with someone who is in no way, shape or form tech savvy! His patience probably saved my insanity... though may have cost his.

To those who have read all or part of this book in order to write a testimonial, I thank you for your kind sentiments. I understand it wouldn't have been an easy read, and may have even disturbed 'sleeping dogs', so to speak. Your efforts won't go unrewarded.

To my children and grandchildren, you are the reason I am here today. I am so blessed to be your Mumma and Grannie. My love for you is never ending.

To my sister, Alison, I could not have done this without you. You saw what I didn't see, and you were the first to offer help. Thank you with all my heart. I love you.

To my friends who have supported me in my journey, being there when I needed help, even if it was just a shoulder to cry on and to hear me vent, you are amazing. You are the reason I was able to write this book.

To the many ladies I met in group therapy, who each had her own story to tell, thank you for listening to mine. Sharing what you went through and the strategies you were using to climb out of your quagmire of despair helped me see that there was a light at the end of an often very long and very dark tunnel. Please remember, You Are Not Alone. I will always be here for you.

ACKNOWLEDGEMENTS

Last, but not least, Phil and Biskit, the other men in my life. Your support and love were what I needed as I wrote this book. Thank you, I love you back... and front.

Sosaj, my beautiful dachshund, who helped me get through that awful time until we escaped from our 'prison', I miss you. You may have only been with me for three years before you walked over the Rainbow Bridge, but I realise now you were the angel sent to heal me. Forever in my heart.

Three things to remember:

1. You Are Not Alone
2. Let Them
3. Let Go

Author Biography

Annie is a proud mother of three wonderful children and a Grannie of three cherished grandchildren who, along with her partner, Phil, and her cute dachshund, Biskit, are the most important people in her life. Running a very close second is her sister, Alison, and a small and selected group of best friends as support.

After being a teacher of Students with Disability for over thirty-five years, she retired to concentrate on her writing. She has written four books in the romance/drama genre, a book for each of her grandchildren and her first non-fiction, a humorous book about reaching the age of sixty and all it entails. She was nominated for the WA Premier's Book Award in 2022 and 2023 for two of her books and has been shortlisted, receiving Highly Recommended, in the Midwest Big Sky Short Story competition, 2024 and 2025.

Annie's new book, *You Are Not Alone: My Escape from a Narcissist to Find Myself Again*, is her first book written to highlight domestic violence, which causes immeasurable hurt in the way of physical, sexual, mental and/or emotional abuse in a relationship, based on actual happenings in several of her relationships before the final, pivotal incident.

Fortunately, Annie was able to draw herself up, with therapy, from the very dark place in which she had found herself to work through many issues to regain the better version of herself.

Her website is www.anniechandlerauthor.com.

Annie's Book Nook

📞 +61 0413 539 434
✉ anniesbooknook19@gmail.com
🌐 www.anniechandlerauthor.com

ANNIE CHANDLER

has always had a passion for writing and has written and published eight books, which have mainly been fiction. Now she is delving into non-fiction, commencing with her own story of trauma.

Annie has a Bachelor of Education in Special Needs and taught students with disability for over 35 years until her recent retirement. During this time, she worked with the Department of Education as a speaker to groups of staff at in-services and seminars on numerous occasions.

In her recent group therapy for women who had also experienced trauma as a result of domestic violence and abuse, she often spoke first so others would know they could speak up, without being judged or condemned, to share their story. Although she is not a qualified psychologist, psychiatrist or therapist, Annie now speaks to both women and men's groups about abuse. She provides information about where they may get additional help and provides many strategies to use in overcoming their trauma to start living a new life.

Annie is available to speak to support groups, organization and schools, on these topics:

Finding your inner strength to...
- Tell your story
- Start being proactive
- Take one step at a time

Finding your best life in moving on by...
- Understanding your purpose and 'where to' from here
- Identifying your goals and how to achieve them
- Believing it is not your fault and you are not alone

Strategies to find the 'new you' and keep being positive through...
- The importance of laughter
- Your journey of growth through affirmations and mantras
- Using your toolbox of strategies to free yourself from the impact of your trauma

Help Services in Australia

---◆◇◆---

24/7 Support

- **Beyond Blue:** www.beyondblue.org.au 1300 22 46 36 24/7 support
- **Lifeline:** www.lifeline.org.au 13 11 14 24/7 support
- **1800RESPECT:** www.1800respect.org.au 1800 737 732 24/7 support
- **Police:** If you are in immediate danger, call **000**
- **Family and Domestic Violence:** www.wa.gov.au/department-of-communities/family-and-domestic-violence-helpline-and-support-services
- **Women's Domestic Violence Helpline:** 1800 007 339
- **Men's Domestic Violence Helpline:** 1800 000599
- **Kids' Helpline:** 1800 55 1800

- ➢ **Concern for a Child's Wellbeing:** 1800 273 889 (business hours)
- ➢ **Crisis Care:** 1800 199 008 (after hours)
- ➢ **MensLine Australia:** 1300 78 99 78
- ➢ **Sexual Assault Resource Centre:** (08) 6458 1828 or 1800 199 888
- ➢ **Accommodation Services to Assist with FDV:** www.shelterwa.org.au (08) 6496 0001 1800 124 684

Western Australia

- ➢ **WA Police:** 131 444
- ➢ **Women's Information Service:** www.wa.gov.au/womens-domestic-violence-helpline, 1800 007 339 Interpreter: Translating and Interpreting Service 13 14 50 or National Relay Service 13 36 77 (Speech/Hearing Impairment)

Northern Territory

- ➢ **Sexual Health Referral Centre:** (08) 8922 6472

South Australia

- **Women's Information Service:** Ground Floor, 101 Grenfell Street, Adelaide (08) 303 0590 or 1800 188 158

Queensland

- **Womensline:** www.dvconnect.org 1800 811 811
- **Alcohol and Drug Information Services:** 1800 177 833

New South Wales

- **Domestic Violence Line 24/7:** 1800 656 463
- **Full Stop Australia:** PO Box Drummoyne NSW 2047, NSW Sexual Violence Helpline: 1800 424 017 24/7 support
- **Sexual Abuse and Redress Support Service:** 1800 211 028 24/7 support

Australian Capital Territory:

- **Canberra Rape Crisis Centre**: (02) 6247 2525

Victoria:

- **Women's Information and Referral Exchange:** 372 Spencer Street, West Melbourne, Victoria Mon-Fri 9.30am – 4.30pm
- **Women's Health Victoria:** Level 8 255 Bourke Street, Melbourne 3000
- **Alcohol and Drug Foundation:** PO Box 818, North Melbourne (03) 9611 6100

Tasmania:

- **Sexual Assault Support Service:** Ground Floor, 31-33 Tower Road, New Town 24/7 Crisis Support Line: 1800 697 877, (03) 6231 0044 Mon-Fri 9am-5pm email: admin@sass.org.au

Notes

www.ingramcontent.com/pod-product-compliance
Lightning Source LLC
Chambersburg PA
CBHW061231070526
44584CB00030B/4073